CONQUERING
THE
SEVEN DEADLY SINS

CONQUERING

THE

SEVEN DEADLY SINS

Lance Webb

———◆———

ABINGDON PRESS

New York   Nashville

CONQUERING THE SEVEN DEADLY SINS

Copyright MCMLV by Pierce & Washabaugh

Library of Congress Catalog Card Number: 55-6768

Scripture quotations unless otherwise noted are from the Revised Standard Version of the Bible and are copyright 1946 and 1952 by the Division of Christian Education of the National Council of the Churches of Christ in the U.S.A.

SET UP, PRINTED, AND BOUND BY THE PARTHENON PRESS, AT NASHVILLE, TENNESSEE, UNITED STATES OF AMERICA

Dedicated to MY MOTHER

Whose life was the best illustration I know of the Christian's victory over misplaced self-love and the difficult circumstances of human frailty. Through her I first learned the meaning of faith in God and the joy and freedom of right relations with the Spirit.

My Thanks

To my wife, Elizabeth, and my daughter, Jeanne, for their constant encouragement; to Mrs. Virginia Wilcox for her kind help with the manuscript; and to Dr. Albert Outler, of Perkins School of Theology, for his suggestions and constructive criticism.

CONTENTS

Chapter I

"FOR ME TO LIVE . . ."

———◆———

SOMETHING IS WRONG WITHIN HUMAN LIFE. EVERY SANE PERSON
confesses it. Desiring peace, we have war. Needing harmony in our
homes, we have conflict, division, and strife. Craving peace of mind
more than any other generation ever craved it, we have less peace
of mind than we have books telling us how to get it. We are trying to manufacture peace of mind and peaceful homes and a peaceful world just as we have manufactured automobiles and refrigera-
tors. Why not? We have the power to do almost anything else!
If man is smart enough to lick time and space through science and
the assembly line, why shouldn't he manufacture peace within himself and his world? Why cannot man create for himself the life he
wants?

It sounds reasonable, but this is our human enigma. We are so
often unable to do the reasonable, right things when it comes to
our personal and social living. From this inability comes the pessimism that provides the undercurrent of despair in modern thinking.

The outer failure to find a way to peace in the world is but a
reflection of the inner failure of man. Reason tells us that we
ought to live and work together in mutual trust and co-operation;
but the walls of misunderstanding, distrust, fear, and hate are so
thick and high we cannot get through them.

It is interesting to note that man's enlightenment has carried
him no further than the wisdom of Socrates in ancient Greece,
who said, "Knowledge is virtue." Know yourself and understand

your fellow man and you will know the right; then you will automatically do it. There were a few ancients, of course, even in Socrates' time, who knew better. One of them, the Latin poet Ovid, cried, "I see the better course, and I approve it; but the worse is the one I follow." It nettled him and galled him, but he had to admit it was true.

Out of the white heat of another man's despair with himself, in language strangely familiar to our day, came the confession, "I do not understand my own actions. For I do not do what I want, but I do the very thing I hate. . . . I can will what is right, but I cannot do it. For I do not do the good I want, but the evil I do not want is what I do. . . . wretched man that I am! who will deliver me from this body of death?" (Rom. 7:15, 18-19, 24.) It would be difficult to find in any age a man more determined to know and do the right than this young Jerusalem lawyer, whose name was Paul. One of the most religious men of his day, a "Pharisee of the Pharisees," but for many years this gone-wrongness within him kept him defeated and frustrated.

Within every man there is a great gulf between what he is and what he ought to be. This is the inner conflict which Paul and Ovid knew, and which all men have experienced whether confessed or not. Walt Whitman bemoaned the fact that man was not like the animals who "do not lie awake . . . and weep for their sins"; but he admitted, as all honest men must, that man is himself a "civil war." It was this same conflict John Milton was describing when he put on the lips of Satan, "I . . . myself am hell."

To answer this basic human problem of how to close the gap between our knowledge and our acts, as clearly and adequately as possible, is the purpose of this book. As the song in a Broadway musical put it, "How can I be what I ain't?"

What Is "This . . . Death"?

For the apostle Paul "this death" was something exceedingly worse than mere physical extinction. It was a living death, like having a dead body tied to his neck. The figure comes from the practice in oriental prisons of leaving prisoners chained together even after one or more had died. Part of the suffering of imprisonment in those ancient prisons was the stench and horror of being hopelessly connected with the dead body of former friends and companions.

"This death" meant two things in Paul's experience and may be used to represent the same kind of experience in every one of us:

First, our inability to be productive; impotency in the face of seen, understood, and infinitely desirable goals.

Second, our destructive relationships with ourselves and with those we love, as well as with our enemies and those whom we do not know but whose lives are intertwined with ours in a complex world. This is the "body of death" from which every one of us needs to be delivered.

Not only the international and interracial wars that leave their wrecks on countless battlefields, but every divorce court, hospital, mental or penal institution, yield mute evidence of the destructiveness within man. It is not, however, the frustrations and hurt caused by the abnormal that do the most damage, so much as it is the inability of so-called "normal" persons to handle their emotions constructively. There is a criminal within each of us which may deal out untold misery to our own body and mind, and through us to many innocent victims around us. The doctor says, "Stop worrying. Get rid of resentments, or you will destroy yourself." Reason tells us what we ought to do, but we can no more make ourselves stop worrying than we can by command stop the east wind from blowing. The wind quits blowing only when the barometric pressure changes, and some great change must come within us before we can live under the terrific pressures of modern life. We desire to be integrated persons using the emotional drives within us for creative accomplishments, but we are unable. Reason tells us what to do to have a peaceful home and world, but for some strange reason we and millions like us are unable to do it. This failure to be the creative, productive persons we could have been; this impotency in the face of worthy goals—this is the "death" that

11

curses the life of mankind and threatens every one of us and our loved ones.

There have been numerous attempts to answer our question since the time of Socrates' famous advice "Know thyself." Were he living today, he would be grateful for the light thrown on man's understanding of himself by modern clinical psychiatry. It could surely be said that man has gone further in the past fifty years in the direction of knowing himself, or at least in discovering the tools by which he might better understand himself, than in any previous five hundred years. The effective psychiatrist could in all sincerity answer this cry, "I do not understand myself!" by saying, "Yes, that is your trouble. You are immature. Let us help you see the reason for the darkness within you, untangle your conflicting motivations, and help you 'grow up.' 'Dare to know' and 'trust your knowledge.' "

Geneticists approach the problem from a different angle. "It is in your genes—you are what you are because of your grandparents." Physiologists add "or your glands." Sociologists hold it is improper adjustments to unhealthy environment. Educators would add "and improper training." Doubtless these answers hold part of the truth; but down under all their helpful explanations there is still what the Bible calls "sin," a word which in this modern day, even among many professing Christians, has lost its meaning. I have no interest in doing battle for a word; but I am intensely interested in the reality of human experience which this word "sin," taken from the Hebrew-Christian tradition, has represented.

Man is a sinner. This is the disease which causes most of the symptoms of moral and spiritual impotency, frustration, and defeat in human life. Unless we can understand this fact, we will never understand ourselves nor win the victory over the major symptoms of our disease which in history have been called the "seven deadly sins."

First, it must be clear that Sin [1] is not just ignorance. Knowledge

[1] For convenience and clarity in this discussion the difference in *Sin* as the cause of man's impotency and destructiveness, and the *sins* which result will be designated by the use of capital letters.

is not the equivalent of virtue, though much of the evil in humanity is from lack of understanding. Jesus recognized this in his noble prayer on the cross, "Father, forgive them; for they know not what they do" (Luke 23:34). And yet it is not the things we do not understand that cause our greatest trouble, so much as it is our unwillingness to do what we know is right and a deep-seated determination to justify ourselves in wrong because we desire it that way. The question is, why do we want it that way?

Sin is not just "missing the mark," as the root meaning of the New Testament word for sin describes it, though it is true, as psychologists point out, that the average person realizes only one twentieth of his capacity. Neither is Sin immaturity—the inability to handle the negative emotions of anger and fear and their kindred feelings. Nor is Sin the destructiveness causing us to hurt ourselves and others. Nor, again, is Sin the disobedience to the Law, as the Pharisees taught. These are not Sin but the *results* of Sin, the symptoms of the disease itself.

Sin is that within us which causes us to miss the mark, even when we see it; that keeps us immature even though wanting maturity; that keeps us impotent and destructive even though we desire to be potent and productive.

What Is This Sin?

Jesus shocked the religious world of his day by giving a new definition of Sin: "Whoever would save his life will lose it" (Mark 8:35). Sin according to him is *misplaced self-love seeking to save my own picture of the desirable in life. It is self-will refusing to accept the relationship with the Father and his family. It is self-sufficiency insisting on my own way and daring to believe that I can reach my self-chosen goals in my own strength.*

Jesus illustrated in numerous ways this new and revolutionary insight into our human predicament and the deliverance God promised. For instance, when the rich young ruler came running to him with the question, "What must I do to inherit eternal life?" Jesus saw that so long as he was obsessed with his own picture of him-

13

self as the rich ruler, he could never be a free, creative person. He had kept all the commandments from his youth up, but Jesus understood his basic sickness and made the drastic proposal necessary to change his "heart" so that the gift of eternal life could be accepted: "Sell what you have, and come, follow me." "He went away sorrowful; for he had great possessions"—and his best-loved possession was his love of himself as the rich ruler. (Mark 10:17-22.) To another ruler of the Jews, Nicodemus, Jesus gave a similar answer, "Unless one is born anew, he cannot see the kingdom of God" (John 3:3); that is, a change must take place in your fundamental affections and deepest longings that can be described only as a "new birth." He pictured the rich fool enamored with his self-picture as he cried, in effect, "What shall *I* do with *my* barns, *my* crops—*my* soul?" (Luke 12:16-19). He told the story of the son who said, in effect, to his father, "Give *me* what is *mine* and let *me* do with it as *I* please" (Luke 15:12). Simon Peter had exchanged his picture of life as the biggest fisher of fish on Lake Galilee for a picture of himself as the biggest fisher of men in the new kingdom Jesus was to establish. When he blustered that his Master must not go to the cross, Jesus put his finger on Peter's Sin: "Get behind me, Satan! For you are not on the side of God, but of men." (Mark 8:33.)

What is the matter with me? Jesus' clear answer would be to point out over and over, as he did to the men and women of his day, that in so far as I am anxious, resentful, self-conscious, morally and spiritually impotent and destructive, it is the result of my refusal to accept my place as a creature, a son in my Father's house, and my attempt to set myself up as the creator of my own destiny, the savior of my own life, and the determiner of my own way. The sickness of human life, in you and in me, is the excessive and misplaced self-love that makes me reject the truth about myself and life and causes me to miss the mark set by my Creator.

Sin is described as misplaced self-love to indicate that it is rooted in the will and the affections and not just in a failure to grasp intellectually the nature of truth and right. William Temple

14

said: "My mind believes, my conscience approves, my heart applauds, but my heart is also set on too much else to trust effectively."

Dante's insight was true when he pictured Virgil in Purgatory pausing to explain to the poet the origin of sin. All man's deeds, good and bad, said Virgil, arise from the "love of good." When this love of good seeks

> The primal blessings, or with measure due
> The inferior, no delight, that flows from it,
> Partakes of ill. But let it warp to evil,
> Or with more ardour than behoves, or less,
> Pursue the good; the thing created then
> Works 'gainst its Maker.

Jesus approached the question of what made some men find life and others lose it from this same viewpoint. When he said, "Whoever would save his life will lose it, and whoever loses his life for my sake will find it" (Matt. 16:25), the obvious conclusion is that both those who find and those who lose true life desire life, or to use a stronger term, *love* life. The difference in people is not that some love life and some do not, but that in some the love is misplaced and "warp[ed] to evil." They pursue the good "with more ardour than behoves, or less"—or they pursue the evil because they think it is good. "However (good or) meansoever anything be," declares the author of *Imitation of Christ*, "if it is inordinately loved and regarded, it keeps back the soul from the chiefest Good, and corrupts it." The story of Adam and Eve is symbolic in its declaration that the temptation to eat of the forbidden fruit came in the form of the good; they "saw that the tree was good for food, and that it was a delight to the eyes, and that the tree was to be desired to make one wise" (Gen. 3:6). No one chooses anything, however evil, unless he believes it "good" for him. Even the final act of escaping life in suicide could be said to be man's act of choosing what he feels is the good for him, or his loved ones, under his frustrated circumstances. *Sin is loving* my picture of the good so that I miss the highest good and, sooner or later, even what I think is good.[2]

To illustrate what Jesus meant by this Sin of misplaced self-love: If the deepest assumptions, both conscious and unconscious, determining my acts declare, "I must have material plenty or I cannot live," or, "I must have people look up to me and recognize my superiority," or, "I cannot live without my John," or, "I must have health, and there is no use to live without it," I am setting up my own idea of the good which I love more than anything else. As long as these demands are made, I am unable to see the realities of my situation, which we may call God's picture of my true life. If I love comforts, recognition, health, and the presence of "my John" excessively, inordinately, though all these things I desire for myself and my loved ones are good, the love of them becomes sinful and prevents me from acting creatively, with true wisdom, courage, and love. Instead I am subject to the numerous progeny of little and big "sins," which are really the symptoms of my disease, and which by degrees destroy me and those I love.

Always in dealing with our sickness we need to keep the difference between Sin and symptom of Sin in mind, and it will do no good to attack the symptom without dealing effectively with the disease which causes it. Note the two groups into which, in general, these symptoms may be divided:

First, the sins of inordinate self-exaltation: pride, envy, anger, hate, avarice, jealousy, and sometimes lust and gluttony.

Second: the sins of self-hating abasement, in which the ego-king on the throne of my life tries to abdicate in self-forgetfulness through the sins of dejection, gluttony, lust, and sometimes avarice.

There is a deliverance from "this death." There are a creative life, a spiritual health, and a productive peace which may be experienced more and more by every person; but it is not through gritting my teeth and determining to substitute the virtues for my vices. This was the method of the Pharisees: do good, obey the

[2] The difference between a healthy self-love and a warped, misplaced self-love will be clearly distinguished in the succeeding pages.

written and unwritten laws of God, and you will be right. Too many of us have not gone beyond this method and are still where Paul was before he began to win the victory.

The Sins and the Sin

It is a sad task to trace through Christian history the ebb and flow of man's attempt to evade his true relationship with God and the corresponding failure to understand the meaning of Sin and its exceeding sinfulness. This task should be done, briefly at least, to give proper background for our personal understanding as we proceed with our own dilemma. Paul understood that the "wages of Sin is death" (Rom. 6:23), but by the sixth century the emphasis was again being placed on *sins*, much as the Pharisees in the time of Jesus had regarded certain acts as the source of evil— though the sins of the Middle Ages possessed an inwardness not characterized by the Pharisaical code. It was Gregory the Great who first listed authoritatively the classic list of the seven deadly sins: pride, envy, anger, dejection, avarice, gluttony, and lust. Set over against these was a corresponding list of the seven virtues: humility, love, patience, viligance, generosity, abstinence, and chastity. The sins were to be overcome by practicing the opposite virtues. The *Penitentials*, and other similar books of guidance, were intended to give direction to those who would overcome these deadly sins; and the seven penitential psalms were matched against them. Religion again became a system of merit by which one endeavored through the practice of virtue to overcome evil and keep the good pleasure of God.

It was this system of nicely balanced virtues and vices, with the sale of indulgences by which one might safely have more vice than virtue, that led to the Protestant Reformation in which Luther and Calvin and the other reformers re-emphasized Augustine's and Paul's understanding of the one Sin of pride, or misplaced self-love, from which all the sins came as the children of necessity. Yet, again, it was not long until the sins became diluted or misunderstood by the Protestant emphasis on sin as a refusal to believe

17

certain intellectual propositions concerning God as revealed in Christ, rather than as a refusal of fellowship and obedience to the Spirit of God as revealed in Christ. As a result Sin became a failure in orthodoxy, and sins were defined according to whatever social mores were considered most important in the local community. Thus many of us grew up to regard sin as certain specific acts such as drinking, gambling, card playing, adultery, breaking the Sabbath, stealing, murder, and other vices frowned on by the particular community in which we lived; while other sins, included in the classic list, such as spiritual pride, envy, anger, and lack of charity and concern for others were either unrecognized or neglected in the regular denunciations which made up a good part of the preaching. Again it was a case of the pot calling the kettle black. "We damn the sins we have no mind to," rebuked Oscar Wilde, who himself had suffered excommunication from society for being guilty of a sin not socially approved. It was a great deal worse to get drunk than to get angry, and adultery was much more deadly than spiritual pride. Again we were weighing our sins and balancing them with what we hoped would be a greater amount of virtue. And though the salvation preached was by "grace through faith" and not by "works," this salvation was regarded as something pretty largely in the future after death; while man sought in the present life to deliver himself—occasionally with God's help—from the customary sins of his day.

It is entirely false to believe that if you are having trouble with pride, all you need to do is to practice humility. Or if you are having trouble with envy, to practice charity; or if you have an ugly temper or a bad habit of avarice or jealousy, simply command yourself to be patient, self-controlled, and to love unselfishly. We may succeed in part; but always, like Paul, there is a deadly drag within us, something that cancels our best efforts. Who then can deliver us from the body of this death?

Psychiatrists cannot do it. They can help, but without the aid of true religion they can at best only patch up our self-sufficiency for a while. Clinical psychiatry, as one leading psychiatrist, Fritz

Künkel, pointed out, is valuable in showing us the "unwholesome-ness of our darkness" and how we got that way. It may be the first ray of hope for abnormal minds. And to normal minds

it shows why all ways that lead into darkness must necessarily be im-passable; . . . but it has not the power to make men turn about, it can only prove in what respect the direction is false and how it must neces-sarily lead into greater and greater distress. In this way it can strengthen man's desires to turn about. The conversion (however) can be forced neither by self-education nor by psychotherapy. Here the practical experi-ence of science agrees with the teaching of Christianity: Conversion comes by Grace . . . Religion . . . is man's only possibility to adjust him-self to the light.[3]

This position can be reinforced by the testimony of numerous other leaders in the field of mental health, including C. J. Jung [4] and some of the foremost psychiatrists of our day.[5]

Neither can a change of environment save us from the gone-wrongness within. Sociologists have a great mission to perform as long as there are slums and sewers in the life of our times, as long as there are those without sufficient bread, clothing, and warmth. But a change of environment does not save us from ourselves. Noah found this out. After building the ark and saving his family from the flood, this noble man found himself in a new world with no evil environment. All the old wickedness was destroyed, but the first thing Noah did was to get roaring drunk and afterward to curse his sons for making sport of him.

Education, knowledge, understanding, are needful; but deliver-ance from "this death" that throttles and enslaves and binds like a dead body chained about one's neck is not from knowledge alone, any more than one's knowledge that he has a certain disease is automatically the cure for that disease. Sometimes, it is true,

[3] *God Helps Those* (New York: Ives Washburn, 1931). Used by permission of the publisher.
[4] *Modern Man in Search of a Soul* (New York: Harcourt, Brace & Co., 1933).
[5] See Alphonse Maeder, *Ways to Psychic Health* (New York: Chas. Scribner's Sons, 1953).

hysteria, fainting spells, paralysis, and other physical and emotional symptoms are immediately cleared up by a revelation of the traumatic conditions under which this particular response came into being. And yet I have on several occasions counseled with individuals who had been helped by a psychiatrist to see the cause of their neuroses but were not thereby able to overcome them. They were still in the old round of impotency and frustration.

Let me tell here a story as a composite illustration of this all-too-usual occurrence among those who go to psychiatrists for help without at the same time the intelligent devotion of mature Christian faith.

She was a regular churchgoer, with an inherited faith which she had never questioned until she began to have acute fears without any reasonable basis, accompanied by fainting spells. She prayed, but her fears grew. She had been going to a psychiatrist for nearly two years. He had led her to see the cause of her trouble. Her sister was living in her home, and she was jealous of her without admitting it. There had been no reasons really for her to doubt her husband's loyalty, but the presence of her attractive sister developed a deep feeling of insecurity. She was envious of her sister's ability to sing, yet she could not admit her sharp antagonism because she was "too good a person" to hate her sister. The repressed guilt over this hate and antagonism was responsible for the fainting spells and acute fears. She understood her trouble and had for six months, but she was no better. She could not make herself secure and at one with her sister. The psychiatrist was right in saying she could not remove the symptoms until she had removed the cause, but mere knowledge of the cause was not the cure. This woman was defeated by her own goodness. Perhaps we should call her "Mrs. Evil-Good." How many evil-goods there are all about us! Jesus' sharpest denunciations were for those whose good was so rigid and self-centered that it became evil.[6] Why was she unable to get jealousy, envy, and hate, with their resulting guilt, out of her

---

[6] A treatment of this tragic note—the evil in our good—will be found in Chapter II on pride.

mind? Because she was doing nothing to get at the basic cause of her unremoved guilt: her Sin. Only when she began to do this effectively, did she begin to get well.

Deliverance: Life Out of Death

"I can neither write nor tell of what sort of exaltation the triumph of the Spirit is," declared Jakob Boehme. "It can be compared with nought but that when in the midst of death life is born, and it is like the resurrection of the dead."

In the midst of death life is born! This is as much a fact of human experience as is the opposite fact of "this death." Mrs. Evil-Good may not have found it. Many readers may not have experienced it. But it is there, forever there, like the Rock of Gibraltar, standing white and hopeful above the raging ocean of man's folly, futility, and impotence. To the lost mariner's despairing eyes this Rock gleams with the light of more sound hope than anything he has ever seen in the changing relativism of wind, waves, clouds, and darkness by which, heretofore, he has tried to set his course. The most hopeful fact of history is that, beginning with Peter and Paul and stretching across the centuries, thousands of persons have found "life out of death" that could be compared only to a resurrection. This is not simply a figure of speech. It is a fact of the transformation of human personality which is at the same time our hope and our despair: our hope—for it would keep us seeking until we find; our despair—for those who know the words of the deliverance but not the meaning of the power thereof.

"Wretched man that I am! who will deliver me from this body of death?" cried the young Saul, storm-swept by waves of evil within him that canceled the good he had sought and brought him to his desperate question. True, the record of the book of Acts does not say when he first asked the question. It could have been that terrible day when he stood consenting to the death of Stephen, watching the stones make their marks on his forehead until he was dead; and Saul knew that it was *his* quest for righteousness that was responsible. Strange that two men had to die before he could bring

21

himself to seek any deliverance beyond his own smartness and strength! He had been trying to do right, but everything was going wrong. The record does say that it was hours later, as he trudged with despair in his heart down the Damascus road, that he saw a light shining on the rock of his deliverance and met his Deliverer face to face. It was a spiritual encounter which he never forgot. One thing seemed clear from the things he said about his experience in later years: he did not find deliverance until he had arrived at the full realization of "this death" to which his Sin had led him —a realization which seized upon him in the moment when he was found by the Spirit of God, the "Hound of Heaven," who had been seeking him through all his Sin and failure. (See Acts 9:1-19.)

"Who are you? Are you the Lord?" he cried in bewilderment.

"I am Jesus, whom you are persecuting," came the simple answer.

Thus began a new relationship, not just with the Spirit of a crucified Jesus, but with what Paul believed was the Spirit of the Lord of heaven and earth. Here in the dazzling light that blinded him, in the glory and pain of a great experience with God, was the beginning of that faith which led him several times across Europe and the Mediterranean, in prison and beyond stonings, at last to physical death, as he, more than any other one person, laid the foundations for an adequate understanding and declaration of the Christian gospel.

Throughout the centuries this deliverance has continued to be the fresh experience of thousands of persons; but only as the shining realities underneath the words of faith are rediscovered by each one for himself. How often these great words have lost their meanings and are passed on without the experience they signify! It is continually man's task to rediscover the old meanings and put new content into words such as sin, salvation, the Holy Spirit, and even the much-used name of God among Christians, "God the Father of our Lord Jesus Christ." Before taking up the specific sins as illustrations of the great deliverance, we need, therefore, first to confront and understand something of the eternal fact represented by these symbols so widely used in Christian history.

Who Is This Life-Giver?

Let us begin where Paul was on the day Stephen was stoned, as Stephen lifted his eyes to the heavens praying for those who killed him. (Acts 7:60.) Saul, as he was then called, had not known Jesus in the flesh; but he had listened to his followers and witnessed the mysterious and often astonishing results in their attitudes and acts. Their victorious and loving spirits irked him and made him more zealous in his persecution of this dangerous sect. Strangest and most unreasonable of all, Saul must have thought as he made his way along the lonely road to Damascus, was their claim that Jesus was not dead, but alive! It was not only mystifying but revolting to Saul's tidy intellect. He had heard them preach their "good news" that this one who died on a crude Roman cross was Christ, the Lord of heaven and earth. Could it be true that this was Jesus whom he had been persecuting? The realization brought a spiritual and mental shock so great that he went physically blind for three days, and his sight was restored only after an aged Christian in the street called Straight had helped him to accept the forgiveness and love of the Deliverer.

For some years in the desert of Arabia he struggled with this new understanding of God. Through continuous prayer and communion he began at last to feel at home in the new relationship of trusting love until in later years it was natural for him to cry in thankfulness, "For me to live is Christ" (Phil. 1:21).

As he wrote his experience to the Roman Christians, it was with a song of amazement with which he perpetually lived. Recalling the bitterness of the old question, he wrote it out again, "Who will deliver me?" and his answer came with fresh astonishment: "Thanks be to God through Jesus Christ our Lord! . . . There is therefore now no condemnation for those who are in Christ Jesus. For the law of the Spirit of life in Christ Jesus has set me free from the law of sin and death." (Rom. 7:24, 25; 8:1-2.)

Twenty-five times in the eighth chapter of Romans, and hundreds of times elsewhere in his writings, the man whose impotence and rigidity made his first efforts at righteousness seem like the blight of death now declares with joy and gratitude the secret of his deliverance which made him one of the principal channels of new life and hope for the ancient world of death and despair.

There is deliverance! This was his great good news! The Spirit of God in Christ is the deliverer of anyone who by faith will walk "according to the Spirit," in fellowship with the Spirit, who will "set the mind on the Spirit." "To set the mind on the Spirit is life and peace," "if Christ is in you," "if the Spirit of him who raised Jesus from the dead dwells in you." "The Spirit himself bearing witness with our spirit that we are children of God. . . . What then shall we say to this? If God is for us, who is against us? . . . I am sure that neither death, nor life, . . . nor height, nor depth, nor anything else in all creation, will be able to separate us from the love of God in Christ Jesus our Lord." (Cf. Rom. 8.)

Is all this senseless mummery? The multiplicity of words in this connection may be more confusing than helpful to the modern mind. Why should Paul and the other New Testament writers speak with such assurance and yet such lack of distinction between the Spirit, the Spirit of God, the Spirit of Christ, and the Holy Spirit? How is Jesus the man related to all this teaching about the Lord whose spirit is the Spirit of the living God? *Who is this deliverer?*

In our generation these words concerning the Spirit, like the word "Sin," have almost lost their meaning. We manipulate our complexes, but we do not often confess our sins. We believe in God—most people in America do, as recent polls have shown [7]—but not in a God who is intimately related to us. In one of these polls, in answers to questions concerning their faith, a large per cent indicated that they believe in some vague, impersonal fashion in God as the Source of all things, the First Cause, at least, or the "abstract Intellect that designed the atom and administers the laws of gravitation and quantum physics." Evidently large numbers of people today do not doubt the reality of some great Force holding

[7] See Lincoln Barnett, "God and the American People," *Ladies Home Journal*, Nov., 1948.

things together, but they feel no assurance that this Force is concerned with them. For all they know, the mighty It could be blind, unconscious, or just impersonal. How could It care for them as persons? Only in times of personal crisis, when "this death" is too obvious, in danger, despair, or great sorrow, do their minds turn wistfully to the thought of the Great Companion. In such times they may try to pray, echoing the cry of the sailors in Shakespeare's *Tempest*, "All lost! To prayers."But more often than not they hear only the echo of their despairing cry. The English philosopher W. K. Clifford gave voice to our modern perplexity when he said, "I have seen the spring sun shine out of an empty heaven onto a soulless earth, and I have felt with utter loneliness that the Great Companion is dead."

That there is no deliverer and no deliverance except by one's own wit and strength is the baneful conclusion of modern man, who no longer expects any help beyond himself. Having lost the prospect of heaven, he is fast losing the value of earth. A great host of persons, including many professing believers, are acting as if the Great Companion were dead. They might not go to the extreme of Friedrich Nietzsche, who frankly faced the "death of God," as he called it, and counseled all intelligent men to say:

The Superman *shall be* the meaning of the earth. . . . The Superman *is* the meaning of the earth. . . . I conjure you my brethren, *remain true to the earth*, and believe not those who speak unto you of superearthly hopes. . . . Once blasphemy against God was the greatest blasphemy; but God died, and therewith also those blasphemers. To blaspheme the earth, now, is the dreadfulest sin, and to rate the heart of the unknown higher than the meaning of the earth.[8]

This may not sound very pretty, but it is the logical conclusion to which everyone must come, sooner or later, who has lost the conception of the Spirit from his thinking and believing. No wonder there are such anxiety, emptiness, and loneliness in this Neurotic Age!

[8] From *Thus Spake Zarathustra*. Everyman's Library. Published by E. P. Dutton & Co., Inc. Used by permission of J. M. Dent & Sons, Ltd.

When we read the New Testament, however, we enter a new and different climate. Here were men and women who were sure of God—not just a purely cosmic God, an abstract First Cause; but a God who besides being the Lord of heaven and earth was the Spirit such as they had known in the warm, loving, dependable Jesus; and this Spirit was near and available to them every minute of their lives. They could have been mistaken, one must admit; but there is no other way apart from this conviction to explain their magnificent living and dying. They were so sure of God and his present love and help that death and suffering had lost their sting. They met the most disturbing and terrifying circumstances that can come to any people with a peace and a productive victory that were the constant amazement of their contemporaries. In an age of impotency they were the most potent—personally and as a group—of any people who ever lived. For the first time in history a little band of people overcame the essential tragedy of human existence by living as creatively, as usefully, and as joyously as the dreams of all mankind had said were possible but as the reality of their present experience had denied. There is much of what the world calls tragedy to be found in the pages of the New Testament, yet words of hope and victory are used more often than in any other book. How did they account for it—this peace and joy, this love for one another and for all men, this confidence and hope? It was a gift of the Holy Spirit, the dynamo, or power of God. The simple answer given by Luke in the book of Acts: "They were all filled with the Holy Spirit" (2:4).

Was their conviction of the nearness and availability of God based on illusion and untruth? To say "yes" would require one to believe that faith in this "illusion" has done more good than all the so-called truths ever told by Nietzsche, and Comte, and all other brave-minded humanists. It would mean that the universe which mankind has found utterly dependable in the physical realm becomes in the personal realm an untrustworthy and treacherous chaos. Some of us simply cannot believe that the transforming faith in the Spirit as the Great Companion, the Deliverer, the

Christlike Friend, is an illusion. Life out of death through his Spirit has been our experience, as it was the experience of Paul, Augustine, Luther, Wesley, and ten thousand other unknown but vital Christians. And this is a description in symbolic words of what they believe is the supreme reality of human life: "They were all filled with the Holy Spirit."

A Trinity of Redemptive Experience

As a necessary framework for our thinking concerning the deliverance from Sin and its death, we need now to have cleared up some of the confusion in the terms used to describe the relation of Christ to God and the Holy Spirit.

Most people in this "down-to-earth" age are not immediately interested in the theological explanation which says, "The Holy Spirit is the third person of the Trinity." They are more interested in the third man at bat in a World Series ball game or in the Third World War or, perhaps, in the third marriage of an acquaintance. Infinitesimal, indeed, is their interest in the third person of the adorable Trinity! But only because they do not understand the tremendous implications which faith in God the Father, the Son, and the Holy Spirit has for their own lives. These words reverently describe a very real and priceless fact in the experience of first-century Christians who first used them. None of them with the exception of Paul was a trained theologian, yet they had all experienced the reality of God in three different ways. They still remained monotheists, but it was necessary to speak of God in three persons: God the Father, mighty creator and sustainer of all life; God the Son, the cosmic God revealed in the human Jesus, their friend and counselor, the "Word made flesh" (John 1:14); and after Pentecost, God the Holy Spirit bringing to their remembrance and understanding the truth of the Father's redeeming love, and coming to them personally in the present as life-giver and friend in whose fellowship they were delivered from the bondage of fear, and sin, and death.

God in three persons was more than an idea; he was a trinity of experience. The disciples had long known the transcendence of God the mighty creator, but in Jesus Christ they became acquainted with his character—they saw his mind, his life, his face, in the face of Jesus Christ. And now in the Holy Spirit they experienced the intimacy of the omnipotent power whose nature had been revealed in Jesus.

The Holy Spirit is the life-giver, for it is he in whose presence the living God becomes known and realized. In his presence God is near, at hand, intimate to man's consciousness; and in him God is also mighty, at work within us to guide, correct, strengthen, and empower. He is near in the fellowship of love and peace, and in the dynamic new and victorious life. Jesus had promised the disciples in their last experience with his risen form, "You shall receive power when the Holy Spirit has come upon you" (Acts 1:8). "Stay in the city, until you are clothed with power from on high." (Luke 24:49.) But this power for witnessing and action is not some vast, unconscious influence; it is the power of the Spirit, a personal communion with the Lord.

Over and over in the pages of the New Testament we find the early Christians equating the Spirit of God with the Spirit of Christ. (See I Cor. 2:10, 16; Phil. 2:5-6; Rom. 8:2, 9.) Sometimes it is the Spirit of Christ; again it is the Spirit of Jesus or the Spirit of God." "The Lord is the Spirit" (II Cor. 3:17), wrote Paul. "God has sent the Spirit of his Son into our hearts." (Gal. 4:6.) "Christian experience is not simply that of the working of a historical memory; it claims, at its deepest, to be a fellowship with the God we have come to know in the person of Christ." [9]

Delivered by a New Relationship

This, then, is the deliverance of Christian faith: the cleansing, freeing, guiding, dynamic result of a new relationship; a fellowship with God through Christ in the Holy Spirit.

Clinical psychiatry has long recognized that it is by man's un-

[9] H. Wheeler Robinson, *The Christian Experience of the Holy Spirit* (New York: Harper & Bros., 1928).

healthy relationships—such as with a domineering or an over-solicitous father or mother, husband or wife—that he becomes sick, mentally and spiritually; and, conversely, that it is by a healthy interpersonal relationship that he gets well and stays well. For the first time, perhaps, a sick personality is able to enjoy a healthy relationship with another person—the psychiatrist—in which he can be himself "without fear of rejection or exploitation"; in which there is no concern about superiority or inferiority; in which compliance, aloofness, or aggressiveness are equally useless, and the patient does not try to "make a good showing." Here at last is one who understands and is concerned, but who will not carry him "piggyback." He learns to be himself and loses his deadly sense of loneliness and isolation. "Therapy not only puts an end to such isolation; it offers the kind of reassurance which enables a person to move forward into painful and frightening forms of self-understanding he would not otherwise have the strength to face." Such a relationship is truly an "oasis in the desert for countless people." It is little wonder that "transference takes place, and the psychiatrist is soon deep in the affections of the patient"! [10]

The fact that psychotherapy does bring temporary healing to some divided, guilt-ridden, defeated souls points the way to man's deliverance from "this death." If one could always live in this kind of positive relationships, where he could be himself, would not need to put on a front, could be accepted for what he is, how simple to be well and whole! Aye, but there's the rub! One cannot carry his psychiatrist with him at all times, and even if he did, unless there were some more profound, divine bond between them, the relationship would soon change to one of anxiety and hostility, with resulting guilt and despair—as has happened several times when the psychiatrist married the patient. The psychotherapist simply cannot take the place of God. No one can—neither father, mother, doctor, nor friend. This completely free relationship between psychiatrist

[10] David E. Roberts, *Psychotherapy and a Christian View of Man* (New York: Chas. Scribner's Sons, 1950). See Taft, *Dynamics of Therapy in a Controlled Relationship* (New York: The Macmillan Co., 1933).

and patient is glimpsed occasionally, it is true, between friends, between husband and wife, or between father and son. Such relationships are priceless indeed and emphasize the fact that healthy personalities are more likely to be found in healthy human relationships. But even under the most ideal human relationships there are depths of loneliness and guilt, of unproductiveness and impotency, which result from our attempt to remove our creaturely anxiety by self-exaltation or self-abasement, which no human relationship can heal. Has it not been the secret of the truly Christian home, wherein this wholesome relationship has most often existed, that its continuance through all the storms of human misunderstanding and egotism has been possible only through a higher relationship which keeps forgiveness and love genuine? Is not this the reason that "families who pray together stay together"?

My current diversion into the way psychotherapy brings healing has been made because it provides the best analogy available to make my thesis meaningful to modern man—namely, that we are delivered from this unproductive and often destructive death in life by a new relationship with our heavenly Father through the Christ Spirit, which is ever near and available to those with faith.

It was this analogy which Jesus most often used to describe the saving relationship between God and man. We are to be sincere in our prayer and worship, as in our good deeds, he taught, "so that you may be sons of your Father" (Matt. 5:45). Nothing is too costly a price to pay for this happy relationship in the kingdom (or family) of God. This relationship is the "pearl of great price," the rich "treasure hidden in a field, which a man found and . . . goes and sells all that he has and buys that field" (Matt. 13:44). "If you then, who are evil, know how to give good gifts to your children, how much more will the heavenly Father give the Holy Spirit to those who ask him?" (Luke 11:13.) His most telling parables were those dealing with relationships between the father and the two sons (Luke 15:11-32); the shepherd who goes into the wilderness to seek the sheep that is lost (Matt. 18:12-14); the good Samaritan who stops by the roadside and binds up the wounds

30

of the Jew who has been robbed and beaten (Luke 10:30-37); and
the last judgment, where the test came not over obedience to moral
codes, but over acceptance of a loving relationship toward those
sick and in prison, hungry, and naked (Matt. 25:34-46). The two
great laws which sum up all the law and the prophets, he said,
are based on love: "Love the Lord your God with all your heart,
and with all your soul, and with all your strength, and with all your
mind; and your neighbor as yourself" (Luke 10:27). Such saving
love is not the obedience to a law, but the acceptance of a loving
relationship.

During his healing ministry the sick persons "fell in love" with
Jesus, to use a well-understood phrase; and their faith made them
whole (Luke 17:19). It was not eros love of the sick persons that
sought to possess Jesus, but agape love that responded to the agape
love they had sensed in him.

A distinction needs to be made between the two principal kinds
of love as represented by the two Greek words eros and agape—a
distinction which I shall follow in dealing with the misplaced self-
love which is the Sin of man and the redemptive love which is found
in the new relationship with the Spirit.[11]

Eros is love whose motive is to enhance the status of the self within
a relationship. Its characteristic actions are designed to control, dominate,
and use the one who is loved. Agape is love whose motive is to enhance
the status of the one loved. Its typical actions are designed to liberate
the loved one by means of the relationship so that the others may grow
and thrive.[12]

It was this agape which Jesus gave to his friends and disciples, to
the demoniacs, the lame, the blind, and the paralyzed. It was this
agape which John saw coming down from the cross as a revelation
of the cosmic agape of the Lord God Almighty. "In this the love
of God was made manifest among us, that God sent his only Son
into the world, so that we might live through him. . . . Beloved,

[11] See Chapter II, for a fuller development of this theme.
[12] Lewis J. Sherrill, *Guilt and Redemption* (Richmond, Va.: John Knox Press,
1945). Used by permission of the publisher.

31

if God so loved us, we also ought to love one another." (I John 4:9, 11.)

It was this mighty leap of faith made by John, and Peter, and Paul, and the other disciples, which brought the healing, loving relationship which they had known with Jesus, their Friend and Master, into a cosmic relationship available to every single man or woman or child who heard the gospel. It was not merely the memory of a lovable man whose wisdom and kindly affection delivered the few humble people who believed on him in ancient Galilee; it was a triumphant faith that opened the door of the human heart for a loving, healing relationship with the great Father Heart, who hung the stars in their places and holds the power of the atom and the sun in his hand, whose character and purposes are revealed in this same Jesus. This is the mighty, awesome, amazing conviction described in the time-honored words, "There is therefore now no condemnation for those who are in Christ Jesus," who are "in the Spirit. . . . For all who are led by the Spirit of God are sons of God. For you did not receive the spirit of slavery to fall back into fear, but you have received the spirit of sonship. . . . It is the Spirit himself bearing witness with our spirit that we are children of God." (Rom. 8:1, 9, 14-15, 16.)

It was this loving relationship with God in Christ which set Paul free from the "law of sin and death" (Rom. 8:2)—this terrible compulsion within him to exalt himself even at the expense of others; to be always in the center of things; to hurt and destroy those who got in his way, by words or looks if not by acts; and all the other compulsions of a lonely self trying to take the place of God. This relationship of agape love between God's Spirit and man's spirit was the "freedom [with which] Christ has set us free" (Gal. 5:1)—the freedom to be our best selves, to be truly natural in the highest sense of the word, free to love others with the same agape love with which we are loved. It is through this freedom in the Spirit that man's creative energies are enhanced and man's highest productiveness is made possible. This was the life out of death which could be compared only with a resurrection from the dead.

32

It is in the light of this sublime truth that we must consider Sin and the resulting sins, and our hope of deliverance. For if man's highest, most healthful and life-giving relationships are with the Spirit of God in creative and affirmative love, then the Sin of misplaced love takes on new meaning: it is refusal to accept and live in this highest relationship. It keeps us from the same kind of relationship with others. If man is anxious and afraid or hostile and unloving, it is because he has refused or neglected this loving relationship with One from whose love neither "death, nor life, . . . nor things present, nor things to come, . . . nor anything else in all creation" (Rom. 8:38-39) can separate him, but from which his indifference and rebellion *have* separated him. Since our highest privilege as a human being is sonship to the Father in the kingdom of God, our neglect or refusal to love God is the bottom of our hell, the root of all our anxiety, hatred, and grief.

No wonder Paul cried, exulting, "Thanks to the Father, . . . [who] has delivered us from the dominion of darkness . . . to the kingdom of his beloved Son" (Col. 1:12, 13). In this relationship only, life out of "this death" is possible.

Chapter II

PRIDE

Into Humility—Power to Be Myself

———◆———

I'M ALWAYS CHASING RAINBOWS," DECLARES A POPULAR SONG. SOME-one should write a corresponding ditty called, "I'm always running from shadows, horrible shadows that threaten me!" Between these two vain occupations—chasing rainbows and fleeing shadows—many of us never get around to seeing, much less becoming, ourselves. Here is a pretty good statement of the reasons for failure in human life: tricked by rainbows and fooled by shadows so that I never become my real self. This is to put in more graphic words the thesis of Chapter I, in answer to the question "What's the matter with me?"

Pride is the first fruit of my rebellion against God and my refusal to accept the normal relation to him as a son to the Father. If the negative rendition of the Beatitudes had been given by Jesus, we might have called them the "Wretched-Attitudes"; and they might have read thus:

Wretched are the proud in spirit, for they shall never enter the kingdom of heaven.

Wretched are the opinionated, with minds closed to the truth, proud in their own strength and smartness; they shall not inherit the earth.

Wretched are the double-minded, desiring many things in their own way; they shall never see God.

34

Wretched are they who hunger after their own self-goals and thirst after self-exaltation and self-pleasing; they shall be unsatisfied.

No one ever enters the kingdom of heaven, where he is free, creative, and in loving relationship with God and others, until he is delivered from pride. Some scholars believe the first Beatitude is really the title to all the others; and one commentator suggests that in a proper printing of the Beatitudes the words of the first, "Blessed are the poor in spirit, for theirs is the kingdom of heaven," should be a centered headline. "Certainly," he says, "it summarizes them all, and strikes the key to the kingdom-music."

It is pride that prevents us from recognizing how poor in spirit we really are. For this reason Augustine, Luther, and many other Christian theologians have considered pride the root of all sin. It is pride that keeps man from recognizing a sense of Sin without which there is no deliverance from any of the sins.

The Vanished Sense of Sin

"Tell me what you mean by a sense of sin," said Reilly, the psychiatrist in T. S. Eliot's provocative play *The Cocktail Party*, to Celia, a young society leader who was on the verge of a new discovery that was to make her life, previously empty and meaningless, full and productive. Through a series of frustrating experiences, including disappointment in the man she loved, she had begun to admit to herself the wrongness of many of her motives. She confessed her new understanding of herself to Reilly, whom she had met at the fateful cocktail party: "The only word for it that I can find, is a sense of sin." In answer to his question as to what she meant by a "sense of sin," she answered that it wasn't "sin in the ordinary sense," that is, "being immoral." "I've never noticed that immorality was accompanied by a sense of sin." She explained that her upbringing had been "pretty conventional." She had always been taught to disbelieve in sin. "Oh, I don't mean that is was never mentioned! But anything wrong, from our point of view, was either bad form, or was psychological."

35

Celia's honest words describe pretty well modern man's sense of sin. He doesn't worry about it at all if he can help it, for anything wrong is either "bad form or psychological." You try to avoid bad form for the people you know won't approve of it, and that leads to a worse disaster—you can't risk social disapproval. The trouble, as Celia confessed it, is that "you either become bad form, and cease to care, or else, if you care, you must be kinky." [1]

A terrible dilemma! And yet soon or late it comes to all self-centered souls. When their crisis is at hand, too many of them give up to being "bad form"—they want what they want and don't care what others think, or they yield to being "kinky" and suffer a growing neurosis or even psychosis. Either way, they are further and further from becoming the free, creative selves they could have been. It is their pride which prevents them from seeing, with the apostle Paul and Celia, that there is something the matter far deeper than either psychological kinks or bad social form.

"It's not the feeling of anything I've ever *done*," sighed Celia, "which I might get away from, or of anything in me I could get rid of—but of emptiness, of failure towards someone, or something, outside of myself." [2]

It is pride which curses and destroys so many of us and adds to the destruction of our world, because it prevents us from admitting this sense "of emptiness, of failure towards someone . . . outside of myself." Pride prevents me from recognizing the "Hound of Heaven" from whom I have fled "down the nights and down the days," and in the "labyrinthine ways of my own mind" in which I have tried to hide from him. Pride causes me to put up a bold front and continue my flight from reality in any way that seems best, and in the course of my flight I leave strewn behind me the hurts and wrecks of my false attempt either to exalt myself or to debase myself when I fail in my ego goals.

Obviously much of mankind's activity becomes an increasing endeavor to avoid facing this deepest sense of Sin. The two ways

[1] New York: Harcourt, Brace & Co., 1950. Used by permission of the publisher.
[2] *Ibid.*

oftenest used are symbolized by the experiences of Paul and Celia.

Like Paul we may try to avoid this moment of despair over our Sin by endeavoring to keep the letter of the law—whether it is the Ten Commandments, or the Pharisaical laws, or the current codes of our community, some of which may be superfluous, but much of which may be grounded in a realistic understanding of right and wrong. No matter how appropriate the laws we try to keep, and how evil the sins we try to avoid, or how much good we attempt to do, we will come out exactly where Paul came out: whipped and beaten in the end, having done nothing to remove, as Kierkegaard calls it, this "sickness unto death" (See John 11:4) which keeps us from the loving productivity and peaceful creativeness which belong to us. This is the way of the moralist or religionist who has not learned the deliverance in Christ—one who has just enough religion to make him miserable.

The other and more popular way to avoid this deep and costly sense of Sin is to do as Celia had done—to minimize and rationalize the sins, feeling that thus we have been rid of Sin. One may attempt to waive the whole matter of good and evil and to reduce life to a simple quest of finding pleasure and avoiding pain.

> The World is very ill, we see,
> We cannot comprehend it;
> But in one point we all agree—
> God won't and men can't mend it.
> Being common sense, it can't be sin,
> To take life as we find it;
> The pleasure to take pleasure in,
> The pain, try not to mind it.[3]

Or we may attempt through a pseudo science to remove the sting of the once-deadly sins, as witness this satirical verse:

> Seven deadly sins of old the Good Life tried to fix,
> Freud stood surety for *Lust*, then there were six;
> Six deadly sins danced a brisk, satanic jive,

[3] Arthur Hugh Clough, "Dipsychus."

Strachey banished *Gluttony*, then there were five;
Five deadly sins pursued their soul-seducing war,
Covetousness? Good for business. Then there were four;
Four deadly sins bestrode the world with devilish glee,
Envy—whom—there's no one left. Then there were three;
Three deadly sins planned what evil they could do,
Sloth? It's lack of vitamins. Then there were two;
Two deadly sins enjoyed a spot of fiendish fun,
The dollar loan abolished *Pride*, then there was one;
One deadly sin—by Beelzebub! the last,
Anger's simply gland secretion. Sinner—danger's passed!
Autres temps, Autres moeurs.[4]

The Folly of Playing God

Pride is excessive and inordinate love of one's self, seeking to play God—the creature trying to take the place of the Creator. Pride is the universal Sin of man—religious, moral, immoral, or otherwise. The recognition of this Sin is the last thing the natural man desires to admit. He had rather die than admit it! It is comparatively easy to confess our "sins." "Of course we have all done wrong," we confess glibly. It is not difficult to recognize the wrongness of a bad temper or a destructive appetite or passion, but it is life's most costly experience to see and confess the reason for our failures: our fundamental rebellion against God.

Seldom has any person admitted his willful, knowing rebellion against God and refusal to admit his creaturehood as frankly as did Friedrich Nietzsche. His position expresses the logical, though unrecognized, position of the pride of every man:

Once did people say God, when they looked out upon distant seas; now, however, have I taught you to say, Superman. . . . And what we have called the world shall but be created by you: your reason, your likeness, your will, your love, shall itself become! And verily, for your bliss, ye discerning ones! . . .

But that I may reveal my heart entirely unto you, my friends: If there

[4] Stanley J. Sharpless, *The New Statesman and Nation*, July 5, 1947. Used by permission.

were Gods, how could I endure it to be no God? Therefore, there are no Gods.[5]

These words are a reflection of that which is deep in every man. Within each of us there is something which cannot except in moments of great suffering endure any God above us; we want what we want because we want it, and we rebel at the idea of any will higher than our own. We may never shake our fist and say, "Therefore there is no God"; but we accept the philosophy of Superman in our own way when we attempt our salvation by creating what we desire.

Ah, ye men, within the stone slumbereth an image for me, the image of my visions! Now rageth my hammer ruthlessly against its prison. From the stone fly fragments: What's that to me?
I will complete it. . . . The beauty of the superman came unto me. . . . Ah, my brethren! Of what account now are—the Gods to me? [6]

This is the sin of pride: excessive, inordinate self-esteem that seeks to be the creator of the image of my vision regardless of the cost. It makes little difference to me personally—though it may make much difference to those about me—that the image of my vision contains many good things, charitable deeds, religious duties; for it is still *my* vision, *my* ego-image, *my* will, which does not recognize its relation to the divine will. I may even attempt to use God, as all religions of magic have sought to do. I may go to church, pay to the support of the ministry and missions, say my prayers regularly, do this or that good, in order to get him on my side as day after day I hammer away at the stone in which I see the image of my own vision. It is this sin to which the first and second commandments relate, in modern as in ancient man: "Thou shalt have no other gods before me. Thou shalt not make unto thee any graven image." (Exod. 20:3-4 K.J.V.) This is the worship and service

[5] From *Thus Spake Zarathustra*. Everyman's Library. Published by E. P. Dutton & Co., Inc. Used by permission of J. M. Dent & Sons, Ltd.
[6] *Ibid.*

of the creature more than the Creator. (Rom. 1:25.) In the clear words of one of the Friends of God in the fourteenth century:

The Scripture and the Faith and the Truth say, Sin is naught else, but that the creature turneth away from the unchangeable Good and betaketh itself to the changeable; that is to say, that it turneth away from the Perfect, to "that which is in part" and imperfect, and most often to itself. . . . Because I will not [yield to God] . . . but I count myself to be my own, and say "I," "mine," "me," and the like, God is hindered, to that He cannot do His work in me alone and without hindrance; for this cause my fall and my going astray remain unhealed.[7]

Each of us has this ego-dream, or vision, of the superman within us. While we may include in it the changeable good, or even God's will, as part of our desires, these are incidental to the desperate urge to create and insure our own success.

Indeed, all the negative, evil acts and attitudes are like clusters of poison grapes around the vine of a dominating passion to exalt, protect, and save the ego-image of my vision; or, to change the figure, to preserve the self-picture which I have been painting since childhood. This *persona*, or self-mask, has been compounded during a lifetime of various conscious and unconscious reactions to experiences of pain and horror as well as of pleasure and satisfaction, many of which have been forgotten.

For instance, a boy is humiliated by his larger and more adept companions, teased and made fun of. This experience continued over several days or months paints a deep shadow from which he reacts in dread and fear and for which he attempts to compensate by the deep determination to "show 'em" how superior he really is. He dreams of many and various ways by which to prove his superiority. These are the rainbows he paints into his self-picture. Much of his unconscious drive as a grown man is motivated by this desire to escape the shadows, to enjoy the rainbows.

All of us have such a false self-picture, compounded of shadows and rainbows, which sits on our shoulders either as a leering demon

[7] From *Theologia Germanica*, ed. by T. S. Kepler, 1952, published and copyrighted by the World Publishing Company, Cleveland, Ohio.

to goad us to bitter resentment, hostility, and even more violent acts toward those who get in our way, or as an enticing goddess to draw us into exaggerated efforts toward achieving the final pleasure or satisfaction. Even among sincere religious persons who want to "help others" and "do a great deal of good," this prideful self-picture insists: "The good must be done through *me*. *I* must be the center of attention."

The Root of All Sin

That pride is the source of our failure is the verdict not only of religious thinkers but also of many psychiatrists. Alfred Adler points out rather frequently how all the ills of the human personality are related to this desire of the self to receive adulation, pleasure, recognition, and so on. Henry C. Link in *Return to Religion* makes the great paradox of Jesus (Mark 8:35) the center of his diagnosis of the ills of man. And in his book *Psychiatry and Mental Health*, John Rathbone Oliver writes: "Of so many, many patients, I have felt that I could diagnose their entire complex cases in those few words of our Lord's: 'He loved his life; and so he has lost it.' "

Chaucer's *Canterbury Tales* has genuine insight when in the parson's story, or sermon, which is based on the seven deadly sins, the parson says, "The roote of these Sinnes is Pride, the general roote of all harmes for of this roote spring certain branches, as Wrath, Envy, Sloth, Covetousness, Gluttony, and Lechery. And each of these chief Sinnes hath his branches and his twigges." Pride is described as a "swelling of the heart."

Each of the other six sins in a very definite way is a child of pride. Envy is self-love unable to permit anyone to excell or rise above one's own superiority, with resulting hate, jealousy, intolerance, prejudice, slander, gossip, and use of sarcasm or more violent means of leveling others to one's own height. Anger is self-love striking out with hostility and resentment at those threatening or getting in the way of the fulfillment of the image of one's vision. Dejection is self-love in despair and condemnation of oneself, resulting in apathy, carelessness, unconcern, and boredom. Avarice is self-love seeking to exalt or to forget oneself in material things. Lust and gluttony are self-love seeking to exalt oneself in pleasures and sensual satisfactions, or to escape and forget one's failures and wrongs. Anxiety is self-love seeking to save oneself in one's own way from death, guilt, and meaninglessness. Spenser's *Faerie Queene* dramatically presents this relationship in a description of the procession of the sins: Lucifera, or Pride, who rules not by law but by policy, calls her coach, which is drawn by "six unequall beasts" on which her six counselors ride. The beasts representing the other six sins are in grotesque combinations of twos, but all are under the whip hand of Lucifera. This is the experience of man in all ages: pride is the root of all sin.

The Frustrations of the Proud

The inability of the proud to organize life on their own is well known. There is ample evidence in human life, and in the history of peoples and nations, of the destruction wrought by man's self-exaltation. The Greeks had dozens of stories telling of the doom of men and women because of their pride. Why is it wrong to try to be as God? Their reason was that the gods were sorely envious and jealous "and loved to cut short everything that overtops its kind. . . . God suffers no one to be proud but Himself." [8]

The Hebrew-Christian tradition recognized the folly of the proud but had a totally different explanation. Instead of making God in their own image, as the Greeks did, filled with the same human traits of pride and envy, the Hebrew prophets in their highest moments of inspiration saw God as the holy, the righteous, whose jealousy and wrath are far different from the jealousy and wrath of man. In the revelation of God the Father in his Son Jesus Christ, Christians have interpreted the wrath of God to be one of the deepest expressions of his love, which causes him to suffer with his children when they sin and to permit them to suffer in order to lead them to himself and the truth. (Heb. 12:5-11.) The wrongness

[8] Arnold J. Toynbee, *Greek Historical Thought* (New York: The New American Library, 1952).

of trying to be as God lies not in arousing God's jealousy but in the fact that I am foolishly overreaching my true capacity.

The fact of man's downfall when he is puffed up with pride is in all literature. God's love is not weakness but wise strength, declares biblical faith. This is that which causes him to "oppose the proud, but [give] grace to the humble" (Jas. 4:6). The prophets in the Old Testament uniformly declare that it is pride that leads the nations to destruction. "And [God] shall bring down their pride." (Isa. 25:11.) At least fifty times in the Bible such overweening pride is condemned. There is something in the very nature of the universe that resists the man who fails to recognize the One who is greater than he. "Pride compasseth them about as a chain. . . . Pride goeth before destruction, and an haughty spirit before a fall." (Ps. 73:6; Prov. 16:18 K.J.V.)

As has been true of egotists in every age, it was the feigned sinlessness of Hitler and Mussolini, their pride in the perfection of their way, that produced their fall.

> From heaven fought the stars,
> from their courses they fought against Sisera

is the Hebraic way of saying that the whole universe was against them. Someone has described *Mein Kampf* as the life of a saint, written by himself: "one who has not one sin to confess, not a single mistake to acknowledge; one who has been the victim of betrayal and injustice, but has never betrayed anyone and never been unjust." And Mussolini's *Autobiography* gives a similar self-loving portrait:

I do not drink; I do not smoke; and I am not interested in cards or games. . . . As for the love of the table, I don't appreciate it. . . . In every hour of my life it is the spiritual element which leads me on. . . . I have annihilated in myself every egoism. . . . I feel that all Italians understand and love me; I know that only he is loved who leads without weakness, without deviation, and with disinterested and full faith.

43

Compare these words with those of Paul, "I am the foremost of sinners" (I Tim. 1:15); and the difference in the influence of the three men is obvious.

A final word should be said concerning the so-called "frank and honest" pride of Nietzsche. Like Hitler and Mussolini and countless individuals in every day, though more openly and brazenly, he deified his own will. In his song to himself he compared his will to "a star, ready and ripe for its noontide, glowing, pierced, blessed by annihilating sun-arrows." [9] Footnote to man's deepest treason: he went mad and died a complete mental and physical wreck.

The inevitable frustration of the proud holds true not only for individuals but for families and nations as well. When one stands, as some of us did after the Second World War, amid the departed glories of Nazidom, on the steps of the crumbling palace of Nuremberg, watching ragged German children selling for a cigarette or two the highest medals awarded by the now-vanquished Nazis, he cannot help but muse on the truth of the ancient words:

> When pride cometh, then cometh shame.
>
> .   .   .   .
>
> A high look, and a proud heart,
> Even the lamp of the wicked, is sin.
> (Prov. 11:2; 21:4 A.S.V.)

The pride of a so-called "superior race," whether German, American, Russian, yellow, white, brown, or black, will bring shame to that race.

> Of all the lunacies earth can boast,
> The one that must please the devil most,
> Is Pride reduced to whimsical terms
> Of causing the slugs to despise the worms.[10]

[9] From *Thus Spake Zarathustra*. Everyman's Library. Published by E. P. Dutton & Co., Inc. Used by permission of J. M. Dent & Sons, Ltd.

[10] Robert Brough. From Allen: *Modern Humor*, reprinted through permission by Dover Publications, Inc., New York 10, New York.

The comedy is reduced to tragedy when through invidious comparisons a war is begun between neighborhoods or nations or even between members of the same family.

She was a beautiful young wife and mother of two lovely children. They lived in a luxurious home in one of the "best" neighborhoods. But something was wrong between husband and wife that canceled their joys and led her to her pastor with a sobbing story of a home on the verge of breaking. It was not just that they had disagreements, but that their disagreements were increasingly more violent and for some reason they couldn't get over them.

"He says such hard things about me and my family—I can't take it!"

Later on the minister discovered the trouble. The husband, though successful in business and outstanding in appearance, was filled with a sense of inferiority demanding compensation. He had come from a poor family and had grown up with the determination to prove his worth. His wife was from an old aristocratic family; and without meaning to do so, she was continually needling his self-esteem. This led him to say things about her and her family which in turn pricked her pride. Small things, ordinarily passed over lightly, were magnified all out of proportion. Discussions became quarrels, and the quarrels left deep, smoldering resentments. Resentments toward the one loved produced guilt and accompanying anxiety, which in turn brought more bitter quarrels. There was literally no hope for that home except for its members to be delivered from the deadly sins of foolish pride.

This on a small scale is the dilemma of modern man. Possessed with the tools capable of making earth a garden, he seems steadily determined to turn it into a desert. Pride of race and color, pride of ideas and position, pride of power and wealth, inordinate self-esteem of men and groups of men trying to play God—this is the Sin that leads to the sins of national and racial vanity, to envy and jealousy, to resentment and hate. And underneath all is the guilt of peoples rushing headlong into suicidal war, knowing there ought to be a better way to live together and yet feeling helpless to change the course of events. The guilt of the American and British leaders who were first to release the atomic bomb is a case in point. Most of the citizens of both nations felt the act was justifiable, given the assumption that national security was endangered; yet the evil turned loose on the world and the resulting speeded-up tempo of international resentment and anxiety produced a deep-seated guilt which in turn created a greater demand for increased armaments. Not only planes but fears have become jet-propelled. Still the "wages of sin is death."

The Fruit of the Spirit Is True Goodness

Since it is pride that keeps us from seeing the true nature of our Sin and at the same time is the heart of that Sin, its malevolent influence on human life is indeed most difficult to break. When one glimpses the heinousness of his pride, he, too, will cry with Paul in answer to his own question: "Who will deliver me from this . . . death? Thanks be to God . . . the Spirit of life in Christ Jesus has set me free from the law of sin and death." (Rom. 7:24-25; 8:2.) Only in the new, loving relationship between the individual soul and the Holy Spirit of God, and thence to others in the family of God, is this freedom realized. In this sense, therefore, it is obvious that the opposite of pride is not the virtue of humility, but faith which establishes the relationship with the Spirit by which true humility is possible. It is interesting to note that in the list of virtues described by Paul as the "fruit of the Spirit" humility is not mentioned, though in the ancient and medieval lists of virtues humility was usually listed opposite the sin of pride. The word nearest to humility in the list is "goodness."

Goodness, like humility, for most Western men has come to have an ugly and undesirable connotation. Goodness has been associated with righteousness, and both call to the modern mind the rigidity and unlovableness of those in every age who have, like the Pharisees, used their good deeds and righteous acts as evidences of superiority over others. Too many Christians have merely substituted a self-righteous shell for a pleasure shell, or a material-possessions shell. They are guilty of the identical sin of their sensual-loving, power-loving, thing-loving neighbors. Too often their prayers and their goodness have been to "be seen of men," or at least to be seen of themselves. It is pride that has ruined the word "goodness" as well as "humility" for most people. Even Benjamin Franklin placed humility at the bottom of his list of desirable qualities, and who today wants to be good, or righteous?

And yet there is a true goodness, a Christlike humility, which is more to be desired than any earthly quality or possession. The two words "goodness" and "humility" are needed to describe the spirit of man who finds deliverance from pride in the fellowship of the eternal. If these words cannot be redeemed, some other word will need to be coined. The basic idea of goodness is "that which is fitting, that which belongs, that which is appropriate," "fulfilling the purpose of its creation, therefore infinitely desirable and attractive, possessing true excellence or merit." The important question is whether I seek my goodness according to the image of my vision or whether I seek to discover and to realize the true goodness which belongs to reality, God's goodness, in which every part of my life truly fits, in which I belong as the bird belongs to the air and the fish to the sea. True goodness, therefore, as I am using the word, denotes the ability to fulfill the purposes of the Creator with resulting rightness, the happy and joyful sense of belonging to the family of God, of being "part-takers" with the divine nature.

The ability to see the true goodness of God for me and my world is the basic meaning of humility, the blessed poverty of spirit which is recognized ignorance and willingness to learn. Jesus was not recommending a kingdom of Milquetoasts, timid and afraid before life; nor a kingdom of slaves, cowed and beaten into submission. There is a world of difference in pagan humility, which is pride brought low, and Christlike humility, which is pride surrendered as one waits, open-minded, like a child before the truth. Pagan humility is pride whipped—self-love now seeking to abase itself for having failed to be as God. Christlike humility is a divinely enlightened self-love and self-confidence on a new unwhippable, undefeatable basis. Humility is standing on the level of reality with the Holy Spirit as my teacher, looking to him for wisdom, love, and strength, and accepting myself and my life from his hands gladly and thankfully. Humility is glad surrender to the truth.

"You will know the truth, and the truth will make you free." (John 8:32.) Free of pride that keeps us forever measuring swords with others or building up our defenses. Free of an inferiority complex that makes us act with foolish superiority. Free of the bitter self-condemnation that makes us abase ourselves by self-inflicted punishment (masochism). Free of the desperate demand to lord it over others which makes us hurt others (sadism). Free of the necessity of maintaining ourselves in some imaginary position of importance which we demand everyone to recognize or else fall under the heavy hand of our dislike, envy, jealousy, and hatred. Free to live creatively, productively, without strain; naturally and spontaneously to be our best selves. Free to enter and live for longer and longer intervals in the kingdom of heaven. What a beautiful and friendly place the world is when I am rid of pride!

Ah, but that is the catch. No man can rid himself of his pride! If knowing the truth makes us free, why can't we set our minds with all determination to know the truth and thus set ourselves free? This is the deceitful temptation that comes to all of us, especially those who are conscious of more than average intellectual powers. Intellectual pride is the most difficult of all pride to displace. Not only Nietzsche, but Descartes, Hegel, Kant, and Comte, to mention a few moderns, have started out after truth and ended up "in turn [by] imagining himself the final thinker." These men were so sure that their thinking was final "they have become fair sport for any wayfaring cynic. Not the least pathetic is the certainty of a naturalistic age that its philosophy is a final philosophy because it rests upon science, a certainty which betrays ignorance of its own prejudices and failure to recognize the limits of scientific knowledge." [11] Why can't we set our minds on finding the truth and thus

[11] Reinhold Niebuhr, The Nature and Destiny of Man (New York: Chas. Scribner's Sons, 1949). Used by permission of the publisher.

be free? The answer is best put by repeating the words of Paul: because of "this death"—this misplaced self-love which produces the closed mind of pride and the warped mind of prejudice. We prejudged the truth by our own personal or social bias; hence we remain slaves to our jaundiced view of things.

Only in the Spirit are we set "free from the law of sin and death" (Rom. 8:2). Only as we come denuded of this passion to prove how right we are, that our good is the final good, can we ever arrive at a higher good than we already know. Thus our idea of final good becomes a body of death hanging about our necks, a ceiling ready to fall down on our heads. Blessed are the poor in spirit, who keep their ceilings broken so that they can see God's sky. "The sacrifice acceptable to God is . . . a broken and contrite heart." (Ps. 51:17.)

The ability to see God's sky is the one thing we ought to want above all else. It is pitiable that we should substitute these little artificial images of our own vision, our meager self-righteousness, so that we miss the sublime and enduring goodness God has for us. Only the Holy Spirit working in us a new relationship can remove the false blinds of egoism and enable us to find the goodness for which we are made.

Plutarch has a story of a man who tried to make a corpse stand up. He tried every way he knew; but no matter what he would do, the limp body would fall. Finally he gave up in disgust, saying, "I guess there's something lacking on the inside!"

For us, too, there is no possible way to make the corpse of this foolish picture of ourselves stand up in the continuing tests of daily life. It may stand for a while, propped up by a little money, or temporary success, or youth, or power over others; but wait until the storms come, as Jesus said, and it falls. There is something lacking on the inside which produces our deep unrest and desperate demand for self-exaltation. And that something is the Holy Spirit of God in whose fellowship there are the insight and courage to be ourselves and to rejoice in it. Among psychiatrists self-acceptance is a universally recognized principle of spiritual and mental health. The only trouble is in finding the answer to the question of which self am I to accept. The right answer to that question is the gift of the Spirit within us enabling us to resist the temptation to try to be the Man-god and giving us the vision and power to be the God-man like Christ.

The Gift of the Spirit: Power to Be Myself

Who can save us from the loss and damnation of pride? "By grace you have been saved through faith; and this is not your own doing, it is the gift of God." (Eph. 2:8.) Probably there is no point on which the divisions of historic Christianity more universally agree: no man can make himself humble, good, or loving; but when in relationship with the self-giving love of God in Christ (grace), he receives humility, love, peace, and true goodness as a gift. One of the most beautiful and moving illustrations of this truth is found in Dante's vision of Purgatory in which through darkness and horror he climbs with his guide to the first terrace. Here he sees Lucifer, Saul, Rehoboam, and numerous others who had fallen by pride to destruction. As the poet listens to their tale of woe and the reasons for their bitter estate, the sense of his own sin, symbolized by the letter *P* written seven times on his brow, weights him down until he can scarcely move. Then as despair seizes him, he begins to hear the "ineffable" voices of an angelic choir singing, "Blessed are the poor in spirit," and he meets the Angel of Humility, who flies near and beats his wings against Dante's forehead. The pride mark is erased, and Dante begins to climb the Holy Stairs, a feat which would have been impossible a few seconds before. "And lighter to myself by far I seem'd." Dante is overjoyed but mystified. Turning to his guide he asks,

> "Say, master, of what heavy thing have I
> Been lighten'd . . . ?" He in few replied:
> "When sin's broad characters, that yet remain
> Upon thy temples, . . .
> Shall be, as one is, all clean razed out;
> Then shall thy feet by heartiness of will
> Be so o'ercome, they not alone shall feel

50

No sense of labor, but delight much more
Shall wait them, urged along their upward way."

The insight is genuine. No one can lift from his own forehead the burden of pride; but once the fellowship of the Spirit with its forgiveness and humility is accepted, the pride mark is erased and all other sins become a smaller burden.

How Does One Accept the Gift of the Spirit?

As part of the conclusion of each of the chapters dealing with the Spirit's deliverance from the seven deadly sins, I hope to give a few tangible, helpful suggestions concerning the "how." While faith is the given which restores us to the right relationship in the Spirit, there is an act of the whole person that accepts this relationship. This is the man-side of faith. Here are three parts of this act which, though inspired by the Spirit within us, are still man's responsibility:

1. The act of seeing and repenting my pride—willingness to see myself *at last as I really am* and not as I think I am or wish I were. This is truly the hardest thing any human being is ever called upon to do. It means the beginning of the death of the "old man," as Paul and Augustine, Luther and Wesley, called it; and it isn't easy to die. It is easy to see the false self-love in our wives or husbands—in others, but not in ourselves. That is the reason we are afraid to accept the love of God. With Francis Thompson we must cry:

I [am] sore adread
Lest, having Him, I must have naught beside.

To accept the love of God is indeed a fearful thing, for it means that I am immediately faced with my pride, my sin. But I can never see my pride, much less surrender it, until I am confronted with the "love that wilt not let me go." It is indeed a fearful thing to come into the presence of that love and to see to what lengths the eternal mercy has gone for me. It means that I see myself in the true light: the enormity of my sin, my littleness and pettiness. I don't like what I see, for I am afraid there won't be a greasy spot left, so to speak. I am afraid I will "go shrinking, shrinking, shrinking" like Alice in Wonderland. It is my pride that makes me dread him; but once I stand by conscious act of the will in his presence, dread changes to love and fear to delight. With the Psalmist I cry:

> Oh, how I love thy law!
>
> .   .   .   .
>
> I have laid up thy word in my heart.
> (Ps. 119:97, 11.)

I hate the things in myself I once loved. I see the folly and destruction of serving the image of my vision; and it becomes hateful to me, so much so that I would rather die than to continue serving it. This is a true consciousness of Sin, which in itself would lead us to despair. But in the presence of the Spirit we are able to see a vision of God's glory in the life of Christ, the true goodness which lies in the path of his will in which we are invited to share. The sense of sin and the confidence of our true possibility represent the gift of a broken and a contrite heart through which saving faith enters.

2. The second part of the man-side of faith is the act of choosing the will of God—God's vision of my present and future possibilities—in which I accept myself in my true sphere. Choosing oneself is the positive side of repentance, "for repentance sets the individual in the most intimate connection and the closest coherence with the surrounding world." [12] A person who is increasingly free of pride "chooses himself and fights for the possession of this [freedom] as he would for his eternal blessedness . . . and this is—repentance. He repents himself back into himself, back into the family, into the race, until he finds himself in God." [13] But this self one chooses is the God-willed self rather than the self-willed self with its petty

---

[12] Soren Kierkegaard, *Either/Or.*
[13] *Ibid.*

notions, twisted values, and misplaced longings. One must be forever through with hugging to his breast either the deceptive shadows or the intriguing rainbows of his old ego picture.

The difference in our ability to be free of pride is the difference in Peter and Judas. Like each of us, each of them had painstakingly built up through the years the picture of himself which he sought to exalt. I have a conviction that Judas was not the bad man who was willing to sell his Master for thirty pieces of silver. I think he was sincere in desiring Jesus to declare himself king of the Jews. He was so sure that Jesus would do so some day anyhow that he merely intended to force his hand. Of course Judas was greedy, as most conceited persons are. He reasoned perhaps, "What will it hurt to take a few pieces of silver at the same time?" And who can say that his sin of self-conceit was worse than that of Peter, who had blustered arrogantly that others might forsake the Master but never he, and then three times denied him and forsook him and fled.

Yet Peter became the Rock, the leader of the early Church, with the costly conceit burned out of him, giving the credit for his wonderful works to the Spirit of Christ within him. Judas, on the other hand, went out and hanged himself. The difference? Peter surrendered his pride, ceased to be a "mirror man" seeking to save his ego-image. Following the crowing of the cock, hour after hour he wept bitterly. He was opening his mind and spirit in utter humility to the forgiveness and wisdom of God, while Judas clung to his pride until it destroyed him. Like Peter, Judas could have returned in humility and found forgiveness even from the One his pride had slain—but he didn't. It is safe to say there would have been no powerful Christian movement if Peter and the other disciples had not surrendered their pride and its false conceit. "They were all filled with the Holy Spirit." (Acts 2:4.)

We, too, are privileged to choose—either the way of Judas or the way of Peter. Foolish pride will always cause us to hang ourselves, if not physically then spiritually and mentally. Faith that opens the door to the humility of self-acceptance will lead us to the victory of the Spirit over error and stupidity as well as cowardice and fear.

3. Such repentance and self-acceptance are possible only in the blessed fellowship of the divine Spirit where love is revealed as the highest reality. It was this fellowship which saved Peter. On the shores of Lake Galilee he met a risen Christ who touched the deep hidden possibilities of the rock within him. He could never forget the forgiving love that asked so insistently, "Do you love me?" (John 21:15). When at Pentecost, he, too, was sure that the Spirit of Jesus was the Holy Spirit of the Almighty Father whose presence was with them in dearest truth. The look and the words of his Master kept him forever growing up out of the old Simon nature into the rocklike qualities of the new Peter. Shells of the old "mirror man" within his unconscious mind continued to plague him, according to the very human stories of his relationship with Paul and the early Christians. Yet each time he was saved from pride by a new revelation of the Spirit of Christ. The historical novel *Quo Vadis* and the moving picture based upon legendary accounts of Peter's last days give a true insight into what could have been the final great struggle with the "old man" of pride with its attempt at self-exaltation and self-preservation. Escaping over the walls of Rome at a time when his fellow Christians were being tortured by Nero, Peter was suddenly confronted with his Lord. Falteringly he asked, "*Domine, quo vadis?*" ("Lord, whither goest thou?") And the Lord answered with words that pierced again to the very heart: "My people have need of me. I am going to Rome to be crucified again. Whither goest thou, Peter?" Then Peter remembered the other times he had needed to be jerked up out of the sleep of self-love by his Master's going to the cross. Again Peter repented of his pride with its demands for the preservation of a false self. Again, in the power of the Spirit he was able to be his true self. He returned to Rome, where they crucified him with his head downward because he said he was unworthy to die as his Master had died.

From that day beside the lake, with the largest catch of fish he had ever made and the first dawnings of a sense of sin in his big heart, until his final victory, Simon Peter was delivered from his pride by a relationship of love and trust with Jesus and with his Spirit. Some of us know the meaning of his victory in our own experience: from Simon the self-loving braggart he had become Peter the Rock. Christ is standing by the roadside with every one of us, crying, "Where are you going?"

The choice which determines our continued slavery to pride or our new victory to become our true selves is the acceptance or the refusal of the blessed fellowship in the Spirit. Otherwise guilt remains to lessen the intensity of the choosing and to nullify the conscious purpose to accept our true selves. The third act of man in accepting the gift of faith into a new relationship with God is willfully, thankfully choosing the fellowship with the Spirit in personal, private prayer; in corporate worship in the family of God, the Church; and in devoted service with other concerned persons who belong to the body of Christ. The "how" by which one accepts the fellowship with the Spirit, and the meaning and values of human fellowships by which the divine companionship is made more real, will be treated at greater length in later chapters.

No one can escape the choice. Where are you going? Toward the deceptive and dangerous reflections of your own pride and glory in the mirror of your own ego-image? Or toward the freedom and light of a new life in Christ Jesus, where "it is no longer I who live" (Gal. 2:20), the self-regarding, self-exalting I, but Christ lives in me—the truth-regarding, God-exalting I, whose growth into the self that God meant is the only way any son can share in the glory of his Father.

See yourself in relation to the love of God in Christ.

Affirm yourself in the pathway of his will.

Accept your freedom in the blessed fellowship.

These are the manward acts of faith by which the Spirit removes the heavy load of pride from our shoulders.

Blessed are the poor in spirit, for they shall enter the kingdom of heaven, where they can be themselves.

Chapter III

ENVY and JEALOUSY

Into Affirmative Love—Love That Lasts

———◆———

SHE WAS A SOPHISTICATED WOMAN, DRESSED IN THE HEIGHT OF fashion, with a well-kept face; but her spirits were visibly drooping. We were seated side by side in the parlor of a speeding train. She tossed off bits of her philosophy without realizing I was a minister. She had suffered, it was obvious—two divorces and a third marriage already going to pieces.

"Love—what is love?" And without waiting for an answer, she gave her own definition. "Love is a sickly sentiment that puts a romantic wrapping on a shoddy counterfeit. It remains only for a few days until it is discovered to be a sham. If only—" and her voice trailed off for a moment into silence. Then she continued speaking slowly, broodingly, as if to herself, "If only someone would discover a pill that people could swallow night and morning that would take out all the nasty temper, the venom of envy and green-eyed jealousy, the harsh unkindness, the stinking selfishness and resentment—well, their love could be real and beautiful. Life would be worth living!" Suddenly, almost viciously, she turned on me.

"Why hasn't someone done that before now? They've discovered medicine that takes out the fever and kills the germs of disease. Why can't somebody discover something that will make real love possible?"

As the train came to a stop, she rose hastily to leave and walked disconsolately down the aisle with her question hanging in the air. I wondered if she had ever heard the Christian gospel. Doubtless she had heard the words but had never come face to face with the tremendous truth underneath the best good news ever told to men.

"The fruit of the Spirit is love, joy, peace, patience, kindness, . . . gentleness, [good temper]." (Gal. 5:22-23.) Here in the divine-human relationship made available to every living soul through Christ is that which does make real and lasting love possible. But it is not something chemical or mechanical that we can sniff or swallow or have injected into our bloodstreams. This blessed experience is a gift of the God of love who made us for love. We may receive this gift any time we are willing to accept it. We cannot buy it or bargain for it; but we may experience it when conditions are fulfilled, as many have in every age. The supreme fact of history declares that, not only the Man on a cross in Golgotha two thousand years ago, but men and women on ten thousand Golgothas in every age who have accepted the fellowship of the Spirit are able to transform envy and hate into love, resentment and unconcern into sympathy, cruelty into kindness, and anger into good temper. This is the love that cannot fail. (See I Cor. 13:8.) All forms of man's endeavor to exalt or abase himself are self-defeating. Envy, anger, jealousy, hate, always fail.

One who is able in the freedom of the Spirit to accept himself as a Son of God—a creature whose creative powers come only in fellowship with the Creator—is thereby able to overcome these and all the other sins which are rooted in the pride of misplaced self-love. Each of the remaining five chapters deals with one of the "clusters" of these sins, or symptoms of Sin. It would be difficult to decide which are the most deadly or difficult to remove. Each person no doubt would have his own order of deadliness in which he would arrange them. Each of us has one or more besetting sins—ways by which his misplaced self-love works its destruction. These besetting sins differ from person to person. At the risk of repetition, it must be made clear that the way to deliverance is not through attacking these sins one at a time and attempting to conquer them by substituting the opposite virtue. For instance, we cannot command ourselves to love or to be patient or self-controlled and always expect the commandment to be obeyed. When we are able to possess these productive qualities as a part of our habitual make-up, it is a gift, the result of a loving relationship with the Spirit. Though one is delivered from Sin as a whole person, it is still helpful to consider the specific sins as illustrations of that deliverance.

The order I have chosen in the discussion of these sins is similar to the classic list except that lust is in sixth place and combined with gluttony as representing the sins of sensuality. Anxiety has been placed last in the list of sins, though it is not mentioned in the classic list. My reasons for including it will be discussed in the concluding chapter.

None of these six symptoms of Sin is distinct and separate from the others. They come rather in groups, with this or that particular sin more in evidence at times than the others. The second deadly sin, with which this chapter deals, for instance, is labeled envy; but it includes those sins such as hate, intolerance, jealousy, and prejudice, which are the results of my self-love seeking to keep an exalted place among my fellows and therefore unable to bear excellence or superiority on the part of others. The sin of envy also is seen to include the sins which result from my attempt to lower those who have risen above me to my own level; namely, slander, gossip, and sarcasm—the tools I use to get even.

The third group of sins, which is labeled anger, is closely interrelated with the second, but is given a separate designation. In this group are resentment and hostility, producing more violent manifestations of our desire to get even, as distinguished from the more inner attitudes or less violent outward acts. In all the sins included in this third group the purpose is retaliation, getting even, lowering or hurting those who have dared be superior to us or who have tried to hurt us in more open and obvious ways. Both groups of sins are costly because they result in the destruction of our ability to love and be loved, without which life is not only boring and monotonous but filled with loneliness and despair. By these sins of misplaced self-love we make ourselves unlovable, prevent those around us from understanding and appreciating the best self within us, build walls of hatred and resentment toward us in others, and lead, or at least contribute, to the destruction of those whom we most dearly love.

When the Bread of Life Is Spoiled

"The supreme happiness of life is the conviction that we are loved," declared the wise Victor Hugo. The conviction that one is needed, is significant to another life, is part of a beloved companionship in which are shared some of the deepest experiences of life, is the first requisite of healthy, productive living. "Ah, sweet mystery of life" in which the "meaning of it all" is revealed! Yet how seldom we discover that sweet mystery and then for but a few fleeting moments! *Real* love, as the discouraged divorcee described it, is the most fragile and perishable of life's riches. It often is identified with romantic love, which blossoms out like the buds on a peach tree in the spring. The next day it is subjected to a killing frost that withers its beauty and turns it into disgust and loathing. Perhaps the bitterest sentence heard most often by a marriage counselor is, "I used to love him (or her), but he killed my love!" Under the moonlight romantic love is precious and beautiful. Under the sizzling heat of difficulties and differences this kind of love is often transformed into suspicious dislike and even hate. This is true not only for romantic love between husband and wife, but for fraternal love between friends and filial love between parents and children, brothers and sisters.

A very large part of mankind is love hungry, starved for affection. The bitter fact is obvious that many of us long for the appreciation and approval of others more than anything, yet we are continually saying and doing the things that destroy the possibility of love. The result is growing isolation, loneliness, and despair. Real love is the bread for which we human beings are starving, but misplaced self-love has soured the bread of life and put a mold of disappointment and death over it. Our very cynical divorcee is but a symbol of the sickness of our day. If the records were more complete in this respect, they might reveal that the lack of *agape* love in the life of the apostle Paul before his Damascus Road experience was a large part of "this death." Scholars differ concerning Paul's marital relations, if any—why he seemed prejudiced concerning women. It is safe to assert, however, that part of the unproductivity which led him near to despair was his inability to give and receive love in its truest form.

> I do not fear
> To walk the lonely road
> Which leads far out into
> The sullen night.

James A. Fraser writes,

> Nor do
> I fear the rebel, wind-tossed
> Sea that stretches onward, far,
> Beyond the might of human hands
> Or human loves. It is the
> Brooding, sharp-thorned discontent
> I fear, the nagging days without
> A sound of song. . . . It is
> The hate-touched soul I dread,
> The joyless heart; the unhappy
> Faces in the streets; the
> Smouldering fires of unforgiven
> Slights. These do I fear. Not
> Night, nor surging seas, nor
> Rebel winds, but hearts unlovely,
> And unloved.[1]

Surely one of the worst enemies of human health and productiveness is the "hate-touched soul," the "smouldering fires of unforgiven slights," the source of "brooding, sharp-thorned discontent . . . , the nagging days": "hearts unlovely, and unloved." What

---

[1] "Apprehension." Used by permission of *Presbyterian Tribune.*

death in life this is! No wonder Henry Wadsworth Longfellow
cried:

> The sole thing I hate is Hate;
> For Hate is death; and Love is life,
> A peace, a splendor from above;
> And Hate, a never ending strife,
> A smoke, a blackness from the abyss
> Where unclean serpents coil and hiss!
> Love is the Holy Ghost within;
> Hate the unpardonable sin!

Of course hate, and the envy and jealousy so often causing it,
are not unpardonable with God. If they were, none would have
hope; for who of us has not known its venom? It is unpardonable
from the human standpoint in view of the costly damage it in-
flicts, for it is the black poison that destroys the finest fruits of life.
"Hate," wrote Emerson, "is like finding a mouse in your house,
and burning the house down to kill the mouse."

It is interesting to note that medieval poetry and drama portraying
the seven deadly sins very often give their most lurid portrayals in
treating the evils represented by the sin of envy. In *Piers Plowman*,
Langland personifies the seven deadly sins and describes their confession. He pictures Envy "pale as a pellet," with a knife by his
side and a long lean face. His body is swollen, and words come out
like those of an "adder's tongue." His confession is filled with reference to his neighbors and members of his family, so "that all my
body folneth for bitter of my galle." Chaucer's parson in the *Canterbury Tales* declares, "In the devil's furnace are forged three cursed
ones—Pride that aye bloweth and increaseth the fire by chiding and
wicked words, then standeth Envie and holdeth the hot iron on
the heart of man with a pair of long tongs of long rancour." In
Spenser's *Faerie Queene*, Envy rides on a wolf in the procession
of the sins. He is chewing a toad from which poisonous juices run
down his face. He is wearing a "discolored kirtle, 'full of eyes.'"
In his bosom curls a snake. Similarly William Dunbar, Scottish

poet, contributing much to the Reformation in England, pictures
Envy in the dance of the seven sins in hell:

> Next in the dance followed Envy,
> Filed full of feud and felony,
>   Hid malice and despite;
> For privy hatred that traitor trembled.
> Him followed many freke (folk) dissembled,
>   With feignéd wordés white;
> And Flatterers to men's faces,
> And Backbiters of sundry races,
>   To lie that had delight;
>   And rowners of false leasings.
>   Alas! that Courts of noble Kings
> Of them can never quit.

As one reads the morning newspapers or hears the story of the
hell in a neighbor's home, or recognizes it in his own life, he cannot help but admit the realism in this ancient poetry. The loss in
modern literature of such vivid portrayal of the deadliness of the
sins is but another indication of the attempt under the Enlightenment to elevate man's reasoning powers to the omniscient and
omnipotent place of God, and the desire to minimize and make
light of Sin in all forms as ignorance or imperfection.

The only modern treatment I know of the seven deadly sins is
a French moving picture adapted for American consumption. The
picture sometimes makes the sins too petty for consideration. The
setting is in a booth in the amusement section of Paris, where a
young hawker cries, "Everybody has sins; come take a blow at
yours." Seven sections of the booth reveal manikins which gro-
tesquely represent each of the sins. When someone knocks a manikin
over, the picture fades into a story of a human situation representing the sin. Following the general French pattern, the sin of lechery
is glamorized and made desirable; and the sin of gluttony becomes
a humorous scene where a young doctor, stranded for the night in
a peasant's cabin, chooses a big piece of tasty cheese rather than
the peasant's wife. Only in the treatment of the sins of envy and

avarice did I feel any sense of the sinfulness and tragedy of the sin.
The story representing the sin of envy describes a beautiful young
woman just married to a noted artist, who is sincerely in love with
her, but who also has a pet cat. The young bride is envious of her
husband's artistic ability, which she does not have. She is envious
of her husband's friends, who seem to share so much of him. But
bitterest of all, she envies the pet cat, which has such a hold on her
master's affections. Her pent-up hatred vents itself with such spleen
that the cat is frightened, falls off their penthouse roof, and is
seriously injured. The artist, coming home, brings the cat back up
to the apartment. When the wife comes near, the cat is still conscious enough to react with fear, and the husband knows what has
happened. Becoming indignant he tells her off, saying that her envy
and hate make her unworthy of his love. The scene ends with the
envious bride losing that which she has so desperately sought to
cherish and keep: the love of her husband. The culprit of course
is not the cat, but her envy.

Not only do we need to see the sinfulness of sin—the black
tragedy in our world and in our own lives that results from sin—
but we need to understand *why* we are envious and jealous,[2] why
we hate, gossip, are intolerant, slanderous. Why is one dejected
at other men's goodness and success? Why is one glad at other
men's harm? What makes a gossip? He or she begins by admitting
the brilliance and good deeds of the person to be criticized, *but*—
and with this innocent conjunction thrusts the rapier home as the
slip or false act is described, canceling all the good in the one
criticized. "I am sorry I have to say it—really it gives me pain to
talk about it—but the truth must be told." But the hidden glee
with which it is told gives the lie to the protestations of pain. Why

[2] Jealousy is often used as a synonym for envy. The two may be distinguished,
at least in this respect: envy is "chagrin, mortification, discontent," toward one
who has some excellence or good fortune I want. Jealousy is suspicion or resentment
toward one who threatens to rival or excell me in a position I consider already belonging to me. I may envy the person who has something or does something I
would like to possess or to do, but I am jealous of the person who threatens to
rival or excell me in something which I consider my own province. Both envy and
jealousy are accompanied by some degree of hatred.

is there so much intolerance, even in me? The word comes from *in, tolero*, meaning "not willing to bear." There is something in us not willing or able to bear with others who by their excellence or difference from us threaten our exalted superiority. The inner compulsion that makes us slanderous gossips, intolerant critics, and persecutors is the burning fire of misplaced self-love in which we seek to cover and remove our anxiety and insecurity by exalting ourselves at the expense of others. Here is the sin not only of the pagans but of the saints! If you don't believe it, just stand around an average group of ministers or religious workers for a while. To talk about you or to reveal my superiority over you lifts the level of my ego and gives me a temporary feeling of security. In another sense it is the effort to make myself more lovable in my own eyes or in the eyes of my friends or family or group—this false idea that by pointing to the foibles and failures of others my own virtues may become more virtuous and appreciated. How soon the envious, intolerant spirit breaks over into intolerant acts of brutality! This tendency will be portrayed in Chapter IV in dealing with the sin of anger.

"It Burns Me Up!"

It is not, however, the openly flaming hates that do the most damage. Most of us are not conscious that we hate anybody or anything; but in many outwardly calm persons there are chronic hostility and antagonism, a slow-burning resentment toward the situation in which they find themselves or toward those with whom they live and work, a hardly recognized envy of those who have more success or more material prosperity than they. They are "burning up on the inside" with the devilish fires of rebellion against their lot in life and the unfairness of God, "if there is a God." Life is unjust. "There ain't no justice," as a poor, befuddled woman who had lost her only child kept saying over and over again. She got along fairly well until she saw another mother happily engaged in caring for her children. "There is no justice," is one of the slogans of the envious. If those of us who are burning up on the inside could "get it out in the open," as the psychiatrists recommend, look

64

at it, recognize it for what it is even if it means exploding in violent anger or taking it out with our fists, we would not suffer so much as by repressed envy and hate. Biologists tell us the adrenalin pumped into our blood when we are angry or afraid is meant to fit us for physical fight or flight; but when we do neither and our spleen is bottled up inside, the adrenalin secretions needle our nerves, develop physical disabilities, and unfit us for life, making our days a rat race. It literally burns us up.

A mother was suddenly left with several small children and without adequate support. Forced to work long hours, taxing her physical endurance to the limit, she began to resent the whole situation. She loved her children. She could not blame her husband, who had done the best he could; but why did this have to happen to her? Friends were kind at first; but as the months rolled by, they left her out of their plans—anyhow she couldn't afford to do the things they did, and who wanted an extra woman around when everybody had "her man" or "his woman"? Added to this was her deep-seated envy of them and their happiness. There was no particular person for her to hate, but she had a store of resentments which sapped the strength she so desperately needed. She resented the loneliness, the hard work, the thoughtlessness of her children, the carelessness and the happiness of friends. She wanted to be loved. She felt it was her right, and she was bitter because she couldn't have it. One day she could go on no longer. The doctor diagnosed her case: "High blood pressure—the beginnings of a serious heart condition." Being a discerning doctor, he went further to discuss the cause: "There is only one hope for you to get well; you've got to quit fighting your situation. Learn to accept it and make the most of it."

Her necessity is the same necessity facing millions today. Circumstances may be different, but the sins preventing love and life acceptance are the same. In one it results in a hasty marriage to escape loneliness and to find love, only to lose it and to hate the one loved. In another it is monotony and boredom in daily work surrounded by unlovely and unloved persons wrapped up in a shell

65

of isolation and distrust. "How many people, even many who call themselves Christians, have grown to adulthood without developing a generous, spontaneous capacity to love." [3] For to love one's work and to love life are equally as important as to love people. Sooner or later every man discovers the truth in Paul's chapter on love: "If I give away all I have, and if I deliver my body to be burned, but have not love, I gain nothing" (I Cor. 13:3).

Love? . . . What Is Love?

This pathetic question of the cynical divorcee needs to be answered. One of our difficulties in understanding the meaning of real love, which is the bread for which the human soul is starving, is that the English word "love" means so many different things. We speak of loving watermelon or "I just love this dress." At times we mean by love nothing more than sexual passion. At other times romantic attraction. Still other meanings are friendship love, love of money (avarice), love of mate, and so on. It is for this reason in Chapter I the distinction is made between two kinds of love by using the Greek words eros and agape.[4] In a sense the divorcee's question about real love would have to be answered by using both eros and agape—both are real—but in the deepest sense the real love she sought must be represented by agape. Eros seeks to dominate, control, and possess—to use—the one loved; whereas agape seeks to affirm the one loved, to set him free, to help and strengthen the growth of his personality. Eros says: You are mine; I possess you; give me what I want. Agape says: You are mine; both of us are God's; I will help you to become your true self as both of us walk together in the freedom of the Spirit. The agape includes the eros, but takes out the poison and the hurt of envy, jealousy, and hatred. Green-eyed jealousy is always the result of eros love and its attempt to enslave the other.

[3] H. A. Overstreet, The Mature Mind (New York. W. W. Norton Co., 1949).
[4] A modern classic on Christian love is Anders Nygren, Agape and Eros, tr. Philip S. Watson (Philadelphia: Westminster Press, 1953). See also Burnaby, Amor Dei (London, Hodder & Stoughton, Ltd., 1938) and M. C. Durey, The Mind and Heart of Love (New York: Henry Holt & Co., 1947).

The strategy of eros is emotional encirclement and capture of the loved one. Sex activity and sex feeling comprise one, but only one, among many manifestations of eros. . . . It is not restricted by sex; neither is sex in its richer manifestations solely a matter of eros. . . . The plea of eros is, "Come do my bidding and you shall gain all that your heart could desire" [whether mate, parent, or friend].

The agape strategy is

to secure emotional oneness with the loved object by means of liberating him. . . . It begins by setting the loved one free, step by step with whatever patient slowness may be required, but always within a relationship which never breaks [no matter how the other sins against it] but only grows stronger as the freedom enlarges. . . . The motto of Agape is, "Go, when you wish and where you wish. Do what you will, for I trust you." [5]

This implies the ability to suffer with those who misuse their freedom but without attempting to force them to do even that which is right. It is to love in the same way God loves.

We may rightfully call this kind of love "Christian love," for it is characteristic of those who possess a vital Christian faith through which they live in the Spirit of Christ. Christian love may be defined as "growing interest in, appreciation of, and responsibility for every person as a member of one family of God." [6] Christian love is man's response to God's agape, which comes to all creatures independent of worth or merit who will accept it, breaking down the barriers between man and God and making possible man's loving response. Those who belong to this family relationship in the kingdom of God possess agape, not only toward members of their immediate family and friends, but toward all men.

Agape is a Promethean fire, which glows in the worship of God and in neighborly good will. The Commandment requires that we live in agape with those to whom we are bound in eros, or sexual love will become erotic; and with those to whom we are bound in philia, or friendship will become either sentimental or incapable of bearing life's strain. The de-

[5] Sherrill, op. cit. Used by permission of John Knox Press.
[6] Paul E. Johnson, Christian Love (New York and Nashville: Abingdon Press, 1951).

mand of agape is not that we "love everybody" in a saccharine pretense, for any realist knows that he cannot thus love human nature, but that we hold in agape (a word which has the disciplines of holiness and the persistence of devotion) even those whom we do not like.[7]

Dr. Howard Whitman writes:

We doctors are learning to prescribe human Love. It is the greatest medicine, but the trouble is, most people—even many who think themselves happily married—don't know what it is. So many husbands are like the man who says he "loves oranges." If an orange could answer back, it would say, "What do you mean, you love me? All you want to do is to squeeze me and take the best out of me and then throw me away!"

Then he quotes another doctor: "To love a person implies to care and to feel responsible for his life." [8] It is good that so many doctors and psychiatrists are discovering the meaning and therapeutic value of agape love; but the mere fact that one knows the meaning and value of love intellectually is no guarantee that he will be able to be kind, patient, and loving.

This is man's tragedy, a recurrence of "this death": Man wants agape love, longs for it, but is so often unable to experience it. He wants to be kind. He means to be, but so often he cannot; for he is bound in slavery to the sin of misplaced love, forever causing him to do utterly unreasonable things and to suffer irrational pangs of jealousy, anger, and fear. This is the reason so many, even professing Christians, have failed to develop a "generous, spontaneous capacity to love." Psychologists have made helpful contributions to the understanding of our inability to love; insecurity as a child, lack of affection, some traumatic experience leaving a deep unconscious anxiety—these are undoubtedly contributing influences to our envious, suspicious, distrustful natures. To remedy it, parents are urged to pour out love on their children, and husbands and wives are urged to make each other secure in their affections. Good

[7] George A. Buttrick, Faith and Education (New York and Nashville: Abingdon Press, 1952). Used by permission.
[8] "An Article About Love," This Week Magazine, June, 1950.

advice, but suppose the parents, the wives and husbands, are too shoddy in their own abilities to love, are too insecure? The rat race is on again. And even if there is this perfect security in the home, the world doesn't co-operate. Their children's security vanishes even before they are out from the shelter of home. Others about them, playmates and teachers, see to that. In fact, a spoiled child can be angry and envious and hate just as quickly as a mistreated, underprivileged child. And the most frustrating experience of all is that of the psychiatrist or doctor or psychologist or minister who knows all these things and yet finds the walls built up between himself and others, including his own family. No wonder Fritz Künkel wrote the book *Let's Be Normal!* with the subtitle "The Psychologist Comes to His Senses," in which he says in effect that even a psychologist has to enter his crisis and find salvation by the grace of God.

What is the matter with us? Well, it is the same old story of man out of joint with his spiritual destiny, of the Sin of seeking to save the image of our own vision that prevents or destroys *agape* love. The envy and hate, the resentment and jealousy, are but symptoms. It does little or no good to repent of the symptoms if we stubbornly cling to the Sin.

Here is the reason for futility in so many people's religion. They repent of their temper, but in a few hours the temper flares again, and they act just as foolishly as before they prayed. They work on their envies and jealousies, hates and resentments, by trying to push them out of mind; but the next minute they are burning within just as hot as before. Something is wrong on the inside that has to be made right. This can be done, not by swallowing a pill or taking an injection in the veins, but by the work of God's Holy Spirit within us.

The Fruit of the Spirit Is Love

"If any one is in Christ, he is a new creation" (II Cor. 5:17), with a blessed new relationship in which *agape* is the natural, spontaneous attitude from which his actions spring. Then he sees himself

69

as he actually is in the eyes of God; he accepts himself and his situation; he has no need to prove his superiority to anybody; hence the root of envy is cut. He is secure in the love of the eternal, and this security he transfers to those about him so that he is able to set them free, for hate is generally the result of fear. We hate those we fear; and as long as we fear them, we are compelled to hate them because they threaten our security and get in our way. "There is no fear in love, but perfect love casts out fear." (I John 4:18.)[9] This is the fruit of the new relationship of those who are risen with Christ.

If then you have been raised with Christ, seek the things that are above. . . . Put to death therefore what is earthly[10] in you: . . . anger, wrath, malice, slander, . . . seeing that you have put off the old nature [the old man] with its practices and have put on the new nature [the new man] which is being renewed in knowledge after the image of its creator. . . .
Put on then, as God's chosen ones, holy and beloved, compassion, lowliness, kindness, meekness, and patience, forbearing one another and, . . . forgiving each other; as the Lord has forgiven you. . . . And above all these put on love [agape], which binds everything together in perfect harmony. And let the peace of Christ rule in your hearts, to which indeed you were called in the one body. And be thankful. (Col. 3:1-15.)

I have quoted Paul at length in this description of the new creature, the new man, because the positive, productive ability to be kind and loving and patient is set clearly in the framework of the believer's relation to the one body to which you were called. We are to put off the old man and put on these new attitudes of compassion and love, as God's chosen ones who belong in the family of God. This is the one Body which Paul describes elsewhere as the "body of Christ" (Eph. 4:12), the Church.

The old man of self-love trying to play God, to exalt himself

[9] See Chapter VIII for fuller treatment of the relation of anxiety to love and to faith.
[10] Paul's word "earthly" did not mean merely the physical, but something similar to what I am describing as the result of misplaced self-love.

above others, to get what he desires, must be put off and the new man of affirmative outgoing love put on. This we cannot do by ourselves. It is not the result of some easy abracadabra that we can say and presto chango we have a new outlook, a new approach to life. It implies the death of this twisted devotion to our own ego-image. It means rising with Christ to set our minds and affections on things above; that is, on God's truth from which we get our values and from which we are inspired in our love.

How Do We Rise with Christ?

There are three essential steps to putting off the old man and putting on the new man capable of *agape* love:

1. We must meet some clear revelation of the love of God in a new understanding of the meaning of Christ's sacrificial love and his relation to our present lives.

2. We must abandon ourselves to this loving companionship in the Holy Spirit, which is mediated through the fellowship of the Church.

3. We must dedicate ourselves to a life of *agape* service; having first begun to love our true selves in Christ, we will begin to love our neighbors and our enemies in Christ with the same *agape* love with which we are loved.

The first law of life according to Jesus, as well as the Deuteronomic Code in the Old Testament, is to love God with all your soul, mind, and strength, and love your neighbor as yourself. What we have failed to learn is that this is not only a law but a method by which the law is kept and divine love is accepted. The law itself is weak, said Paul. You cannot command yourself to love no matter how well you know the law of love and give mental assent to it. "For God has done what the law, weakened by the flesh, could not do: sending his own Son in the likeness of sinful flesh." (Rom. 8:3.) Jesus did more than reiterate the summary of the law and the commandments; he did more than simply repeat that which is declared in the highest insights of Hebrew religion concerning the love of God. In his own life and death and resurrection he revealed the love of God. Whether or not the words in John's Gospel, "He who has seen me has seen the Father. . . . [The Father and I are one]" (John 14:9), are actually the words of Jesus or the words of his disciples commenting on their experience of him, the great truth is the same: "God was in Christ reconciling the world to himself" (II Cor. 6:19). The result of this reconciliation, the blessed relationship restored between the Father and his beloved children, Paul describes thus: "The fruit of the Spirit is love, joy, peace, patience, . . . self-control (Gal. 5:22-23). How, then, does this relationship come into being?

1. *We are saved from the sins against love by the conviction that we are loved.* This is the verdict not only of centuries of Christian experience but of modern clinical psychiatry; it is the security of a great love that sets us free from the venom of envy, jealousy, resentment, and hate. Psychiatry can give the prescription. Only the love of God can fill it as completely as it must be filled, as we yield our confused, divided, and love-starved souls to the divine love of One "whose name is love, whose nature is compassion, whose presence is joy, whose word is truth, whose spirit is goodness, whose holiness is beauty, whose will is peace, whose service is perfect freedom, and in knowledge of whom standeth our eternal life."

Dante in Purgatory catches a glimpse of this hopeful fact. Having climbed with his guide to the third terrace, he sees the souls of the envious, clad in sackcloth and having their eyes sewed up with an iron thread; and he shudders over the malevolent curse brought by their sin as they describe their woes. Among them is Guido of Duca, who wails:

> Envy so parch'd my blood, that had I seen
> A fellow man made joyous, thou hadst mark'd
> A livid paleness overspread my cheek.

Recognizing in himself the roots of envy, Dante is again in the depths of despair and remains so until the angel hails him with glad voice, joining with the angelic choir, "Blessed the merciful," and

"Happy thou, that conquer'st." Dante is encouraged but mystified and asks Virgil what it means. Virgil answers:

> Envy bloweth up men's sighs.
> No fear of that might touch ye, if the love
> Of higher sphere exalted your desire.

No clinical psychiatry, no exalted power of man's reason, can sew up the eyes of the envious—only the deliverance of a great love in a higher relationship can "exalt your desire." We are all familiar with this redemption on the human level. In the words of David Seabury,

> If we would be psychically well there must be a more potent factor than the mere absence of enmity and bitterness. Love must enter as the ruling principle of life. We have all witnessed the transforming effect of mate love. People who have been lonely and quiescent blossom suddenly into mellow outgoingness. The old Mary or John is humanized and emanates warmth and affection, not only toward the beloved but to all mankind.[11]

But when mate love loses its potency in the reassertion of misplaced self-love, what then? When with all the security of human love we are still insecure and no one can remove from us "this body of death," what then? Then, the gospel of Christ declares, the miracle of divine grace may take place as you begin to open your eyes to a new revelation of love in the heart of the Eternal. Sometimes this new revelation of love is seen in the life of another person, as Saul saw the love of Christ shining in the face of Stephen, even as Saul held his clothes as he was stoned. Sometimes as one reads from the pages of the New Testament, the person of Christ steps forth in new meaning; and before he knows it, the very Spirit of God speaks to his consciousness of the love that is and was and ever shall be. Again, it may be in the warm fellowship of a Christlike community whose worship is translated into loving acts, and we are

[11] *How Jesus Heals Our Minds Today* (New York: Little, Brown & Co., 1940).

73

recipients of the merciful blessedness which could come only from the mercy of God. But more often than any other way, the meaning of the divine love revealed in Calvary is understood in a flash of sudden insight as we stand pierced to the heart by the loving sacrifice of One who died for us, who "bore all my sins upon the tree." We may be repelled by all men's theories of the Atonement, or we may know nothing at all about any theory, but in the love of Christ we, too, as did the first disciples, find the suffering, redeeming love of God, which includes us.

Countless illustrations of this truth of experience could be given. One of my favorites is the story of William Cowper, one of England's greatest poets. Disgusted with the self-righteous goodness of so many Christians he knew, he was unable to see the great meaning of faith in Christ which he had heard since childhood. One day, hemmed in by resentments and futility, isolated from the love and understanding every soul craves, finding only loneliness and betrayal, he was contemplating suicide. In despair he opened his little-used Bible and began to read. His eyes fell on the words: "Since all have sinned and fall short of the glory of God, they are justified by his grace as a gift, through the redemption which is in Christ Jesus, whom God put forward as an expiation by his blood" (Rom. 3:23-25).

Something happened to William Cowper which lifted him to a new level of confident inner security and made an outgoing love possible for him. It was nothing mechanical or magical, as if the blood of a man dying on the cross within itself had power to restore him to sanity and enable him to love. Those who are horrified by "salvation through the blood of Christ" completely miss the point. The blood of Christ which stirred William Cowper's faith in an hour of despair, when he was ready to shed his own blood in bitter frustration, was an open sesame into the heart of God, whose love was deep enough and wide enough to include him in all his failure and lovelessness. If to the mighty God he, William Cowper, was lovable, precious enough to permit his Son to die for, there must be something in life precious enough to live and fight for. No legal justification this, but a restoration to a lost love that declared him worthy, even though he had been unworthy. If in Jesus' sacrifice God showed his own true nature, the Lamb that was slain before the foundation of the world (Rev. 13:8), then God cares. Forgiveness was realized, and Cowper was set free of the old man with his envious, proud self-seeking. The act on Calvary was no longer a spectacle in distant history, but was a present act on the calvary of his own failure by which God assured him of abiding love. William Cowper began a new life and as the testimony to his new relationship wrote one of our best loved hymns:

> There is a fountain filled with blood
> Drawn from Immanuel's veins;
> And sinners, plunged beneath that flood,
> Lose all their guilty stains,
> The dying thief rejoiced to see
> That fountain in his day;
> And there may I, though vile as he,
> Wash all my sins away.

Let those who are horrified by all this talk of blood beware lest they fall into the sentimentality by which no human soul is redeemed. In a day when whole cities may be filled with the blood of slaughtered peoples due to the pride and envy of men, it is not fitting for any sane person to be squeamish in speaking of the slaughtered Lamb of God. Indeed "it was real blood ran from His Hands and the nail-holes" [12] just as it was real blood shed on Tarawa and the beaches of Normandy and on Porkchop Hill in Korea. It is the deadliest kind of artificiality to speak in religion only of "sweetness and light" and to miss the cosmic symbolism in the cross of Christ, which is more than a symbol, for it bears in its own reality something of the divine reality it foreshadows. Is there or is there not at the heart of all things a Father-heart that suffers when his children suffer, that goes with them to their crosses, that bears their sins and forgives them because he made

[12] Carl Sandburg, "To a Contemporary Bunkshooter."

75

them to be worthy of eternal life? That is the question. The blood drops from the cross of Christ declare that it is so, everlastingly so! The transformed redeemed of every age declare that it is so, presently so! The answering faith from your own heart this moment may know that it is so, graciously so!

2. *We are saved from the sins against love by abandonment to the blessed fellowship.*

"See what love the Father has given us, that we should be called children of God. . . . We know that we have passed out of death into life, because we love the brethren. . . . Beloved, let us love one another; for love is of God, and he who loves is born of God and knows God . . . ; for God is love." (I John 3:1, 14; 4:7-8.)

This conviction was and is the dynamic of the Christian's love— the wonderful elixir which will produce real love for the woman thrice divorced, for the widow resenting her loneliness, for the office clerk bored with people unlovely and unloved, and for the man burning up with hate. Faith in Christ that saves us from our deadly sin against love is nothing more nor less than the conviction that we are loved and the abandonment of our isolation and insecurity in the warming freedom of the blessed fellowship. This fellowship includes not only the prophets and martyrs who have gone before us, the saints who will come after us, and the brethren who work and worship with us through all the pressures of our daily living, but also the fellowship of the Spirit in which God's abiding presence is most dearly made real. I say "abandonment" because there is no other word to describe the spirit of a man yielding himself to such free and full communion as the body of Christ actually is.

Granted that too often the Church as we have experienced it has not been such a blessed fellowship, has not been the body of Christ in which each of the members belonged in the priceless freedom of the Spirit. It has not been this kind of fellowship for the very reason that its members have not really abandoned themselves to Christ and to the fellowship he offers. Their commitments have been partial, tentative, like a boy taking his first early summer swim.

76

Their toes are in the water, maybe their ankles, but rarely their whole lower limbs, not to speak of the entire body. They love Christ and his brothers but with reservations. They would use the Church for peace of mind, or for strength, or for other more ulterior motives; but rarely do they share that delicious sense of belonging to a great company of free spirits made one by their common devotion to Christ, whose sacrifice of himself makes *agape* love possible. And yet this kind of utter belongingness is characteristic of those who have truly begun to be free of pride and envy, of misplaced self-love and its numerous evil progeny. They have abandoned themselves to the love of God and to the Family relationships. The real church is no formal institution, cold and lifeless, as it is to so many who claim membership. It is a blessed fellowship of the redeemed and of the concerned, from which they draw their spiritual breath, find their ground of steady security, and through which they fulfill their responsibility.

He is our peace, who has made us . . . one, and has broken down the dividing wall of hostility, . . . for through him we . . . have access in one Spirit to the Father. So then you are no longer strangers and sojourners, but you are fellow citizens with the saints and members of the household of God, built upon the foundation of the apostles and prophets, Christ Jesus himself being the chief cornerstone, in whom the whole structure is joined together and grows into a holy temple in the Lord; in whom you also are built into it for a dwelling place of God in the Spirit. (Eph. 2:14, 18-22.)

Where could any psychiatrist find a relationship with more therapeutic powers than this sense of utter belongingness possessed by those who are abandoned in heart, mind, and will to the divine-human fellowship? Where is there a more potent solvent for the hates and fears and envies of mankind? That too seldom our churches have provided such a fellowship is no indictment of the body of Christ, but an indication of the absence of the fellowship— or its presence in too few of the members of the visible organization.

There are two reasons why the Church is not the blessed fellowship in Christ for many Christians that it was meant to be—two equally fatal errors—first, that religion is only vertical, between God and my private soul; and second, that religion is only horizontal, between my brother and me.

The first error is the older. It says, "God and I, the two of us, have an understanding. I pray to him, and he gives me peace and help. I don't need the church, for my God and I, we get along well without any help from others." Such a religion is not of *agape*, but of *eros*; not of the God in Christ, but of the tribal, family, or personal gods we have manufactured for ourselves. It is but another manifestation of the one Sin: bloated, inflated self-love which seeks to exalt and preserve the ego-image even through the use of religion. Such unchristian, individualistic, pietistic religion explains the presence of large numbers of professing Christians without Christlike compassion and concern for their fellows, and provides the basis for the kind of disgust indicated in the statement, "The atheist is only a fool, but religion is the ultimate sin." Such individualistic religion is the "ultimate sin"; it is religion gone sour, and there is nothing more ill-smelling than religious faith which ignores our responsibility to one another. John put it bluntly when he declared, "If any one says, 'I love God,' and hates his brother, he is a liar; for he who does not love his brother whom he has seen, cannot love God whom he has not seen" (I John 4:20). No, you simply cannot be in Christ and be in isolation.

The second equally fatal error is the idea that religion is only horizontal. For the vertical "my God and I" this way would substitute "my brother and I." This has been the favorite thinking of those who rule out any divine presence or influence beyond that which is in man himself; or if God is permitted to exist, he is kept in the distant confines of atomic and stellar activity and not allowed to be anything resembling a personal Spirit.[13] Many people, unable to understand the conflicts in theological explanations which seemed to occupy the Church in their youth, have thrown the whole thing out the window and adopted a simple religion of

[13] See discussion in Chapter VIII on the mystery of the Incomprehensible.

humanism which has as its creed "love for my fellow man." Some call it the religion of the Golden Rule—treat your fellow man right, and that's the end of it. You don't need the church to do that! Some others who adopted the humanist creed, however, have tried to keep the Church, considering it as just one of the several helpful associations of men by which the progress of brother love would some day bring about the absence of war and poverty and usher in universal peace and well-being for mankind. There is an element of truth in the insistence that one never finds God until he finds his brother. As Ernest Crosby testifies:

> No one could tell me where my soul might be;
> I searched for God, and He eluded me;
> I sought my brother out, and found all three.[14]

The pressing question, however, is "Can I find my brother and love him continually and rightly without loving God?" How can you love your neighbor when he becomes your enemy and tries to put you on a cross? This is the acid test which this shallow religion of mere human love fails to meet. It was this kind of religion among many Germans which yielded so quickly to the brutal ruthlessness of the Nazis. When the test comes, only those whose religion is vertical as well as horizontal can stand firm in truth and *agape* love. To the amazement of those who had little use for the church, it was the relatively few Germans who loved God in the fellowship of the church who withstood the Nazis, while so many in the liberal universities and newspapers (the *avant-garde*) were knuckling under.

True religion, which results in the Spirit's deliverance of man from his Sin, can never be the "flight from the alone to the Alone," because no soul has a right to appear alone in his presence. We are inextricably bound up with one another. Neither can true religion ever be merely the linking of insignificance with insignificance, littleness with littleness; nor can it be the mere pooling of our ignorance and weakness. True religion links God and man through

[14] "The Search."

the church, where the alone is made into a great fellowship, where our weakness is infused with his strength, our lovelessness with his love, and our poverty of understanding with his widom.

"For the Spirit [of God] is a Spirit of fellowship: He maketh men to be of one mind in a house. The man who enjoys God most is the one who most enjoys the society of his fellow creatures," and the man who can give *agape* love to his fellow creatures is the one who is self-abandoned to the love of God.

> He prayeth best, who loveth best
> All things both great and small;
> For the dear God who loveth us,
> He made and loveth all.[15]

The other side of this truth is that he loveth best who prayeth best. And the love both of God and of my neighbor is most readily found in the living, vital fellowship which is the Church: the body of Christ.

3. *Love others as you love yourself—in Christ.* The ability to love (or to affirm) ourselves in the sense of *agape* love is one of the results of new life in the Spirit. It is *eros* love of only oneself that is the curse of mankind. It is *agape* love of which Jesus spoke when he said to love God, and your neighbor as yourself. Eric Fromm has made a real contribution to the meaning of such self-love as the positive affirmation of one's best self. He says there are four characteristics of productive love: care, responsibility, repect, and knowledge. The Hebrew term for God's love for man and man's love for man is *rachamim*, the root of which is *rechem*— "womb." Love is "to care, to be responsible for," as a mother is for her babe, without any conditions. However, says Fromm, this care and responsibility become hurtful unless they are with respect and knowledge.[16]

Before we can love ourselves with *agape* love, just as before we can love others with the same affirming, freeing love, we must have

---

[15] Coleridge, "The Rime of the Ancient Mariner."
[16] *Man for Himself* (New York: Rinehart & Co., Inc., 1947).

more than a feeling of responsibility; we must also have an understanding of ourselves and of the persons loved. We must see ourselves and our neighbors in true perspective, as God sees us and them, or we will have a misplaced love, which is Sin. Nietzsche's insight was true, at least in this respect, when he said, "Your neighbor love is your bad love of yourselves. Ye feel unto your neighbor from yourselves, and would fain make a virtue thereof! But I fathom your 'unselfishness.' . . . You cannot stand yourselves and you do not love yourselves sufficiently." [17]

As would-be Christians we must also recognize the fact that when man is unable to love others, he does not truly love himself. Both *agape* love of self and of neighbors grow together in the love of Christ. A fuller treatment of this fact is given in the following two chapters on the sins of anger and the sins of dejection and self-condemnation. The ability to be patient without being cowardly and the outgoing acts of *agape* love toward others are truly priceless fruits of the Spirit.

How do I become capable of loving and worthy of being loved? Not by striving or anxiety, not by any amount of self-effort or self-education—though study and seeking may provide rich and helpful insights of great value—but when I learn to accept the love that is revealed by the cross of Christ and to lose myself "in wonder, love, and praise," then I am able to love genuinely.

One of the bright stars in the dark sky of the late Middle Ages was Francis of Sales. In a little book, *The Spirit of St. Francóis de Sales*, one of his contemporaries describes a conversation in which they were talking about our problem: How does one attain unto the virtues of a Christlike love? Francis answered that it was through the "little virtues that grow beneath the Cross." His friend asked what virtues he referred to, and the venerable saint answered, "Humility, patience, gentleness, kindness, forbearance, . . . calmness, good temper, heartiness, pity, ready forgiveness, simplicity, frank-

[17] From *Thus Spake Zarathustra*. Everyman's Library. Published by E. P. Dutton & Co., Inc. Used by permission of J. M. Dent & Sons, Ltd.

ness, and so on. These virtues are like violets growing in a shady nook, fed by the dew of heaven, and though unseen they shed forth a sweet and precious odor." [18]

This is our good news to love-starved humanity: agape love, and all the little virtues clinging thereto, grow in the relationship of a great redemptive love. Let us pray God to write his love in our hearts and with it all the little virtues that grow at the foot of the cross.

> Here, O Christ, our sins we see,
>   Learn Thy love while gazing thus;
> Sin, which laid the cross on Thee,
>   Love, which bore the cross for us.

> Here we learn to serve and give,
>   And, rejoicing, self deny;
> Here we gather love to live,
>   Here we gather faith to die!

---

[18] Jean Pierre Camus, tr. C. F. Kelley (New York: Harper & Bros., 1952).

Chapter IV

ANGER and INTOLERANCE

Into Patience and Magnanimity—Love That Heals

———◆———

Here we are—the only animals given human speech—and here we are, snarling at each other!"

These words from the musical *The Band Wagon* may serve very well not only as the confession of modern man's predicament, but also as the reason for his frustration. They are spoken by the hero, Tony Hunter, a once-famous movie dancer whose place in the sun in this capacity is rapidly turning into an eclipse. He is talking in a quiet spot in the garden with the famous ballet dancer Gabrielle Girard, who has come to make up with him in order that the show in which they are to play the leading roles may continue. Instead of making up, however, they both engage in a nasty display of temper. The reasons are obvious to the audience, if not to the actors: bitter envy on the part of Tony because Gaby is adept at this kind of dancing and he isn't, anger in Gaby because Tony has looked down on her and minimized her talents before all the cast. In the quiet after the explosion Tony suddenly becomes philosophical, and this is the verdict he renders of their plight: "We are the only animals given human speech, and here we are snarling at each other!"

The musical was filmed, of course, for entertainment, as one of the song and dance acts declares; nevertheless, whether the author intended it so or not, underneath the words are the cold facts which explain the various impasses of anger and hostility, intolerance and revenge, in which man finds himself.

We Are Animals; Why Shouldn't We Snarl?

The evil fruits of our secular age are being harvested. From movie theaters to schoolrooms, from novels to psychiatrists' couches, Tony and Gabrielle and their counterparts in our Western world have been taught for the last fifty years that they are nothing but higher animals, with animal responses, animal instincts; and, therefore, their highest happiness comes only in "doing what comes naturally," interpreted in animal sensations; that God and religion are at best only conveniences for the sake of marriage and funerals, if they are to be accepted at all. There may or may not be a tomorrow after we die, but no use to worry about that now. Today we are animals. We began in the mud; what more could you expect of us than muddy lives and an end in the mud?

With animals the one law is self-preservation. So with man—the chief difference being that man's physical life is not often threatened. Instead he fights to preserve and keep intact his ego-image of himself—the persona, or self-mask, he has so painstakingly built up since babyhood. No wonder Tony confesses earlier in the musical as he lights from the train in New York and the usual crowd of fans is not there to meet him, "I can stand anything but failure!" So with every one of us who is still under the curse of "this death"— the result of his Sin of misplaced love seeking to make himself his own God. We simply cannot stand failure if we are the only gods there be! When friends, strangers, enemies, or even members of the family get in my way, threaten the success of my ego dream, I am compelled to be angry, to hate, to lie, and if the stakes are large enough and I am desperate enough, to steal and to kill. Since the Gabrielles as well as the Tonys all have images of their vision in which each is trying to be a superman in his own way, it is inevitable that their visions should clash. We get in one another's hair, and those we thought would love us (the proof of their love being that they will help us get what we want, exalt us, make us feel important) have turned out to be our enemies, and hate takes the place of love. For hate is always the underside of *eros* love. Failure is more and more to be expected, therefore, especially as youth fades. Even when I am on top of the heap, I am threatened more savagely than when I had not yet arrived.

So Tony and his partner join in a dance duet in which they sing, "I tried to reach the moon, but all I could find when I got there was the air!"

Here we are snarling at one another; because, being animals, strangely enough we are not content to remain animals, chewing placidly at our human cuds or wallowing contentedly in our piggish mud. No, we put on airs! We are dissatisfied, restless, filled with indescribable longings and unutterable dread. And we try to cover up our unsatisfied cravings and to compensate for our frustrations and mistakes by acting as if we were gods. The whole world should bow down to us—or at least our own family should, or our office staff, or those who share the same factory bench, or our public. We try to reach the moon, and all we get is the air.

This astonishingly complete parable of modern man's defeat ends with several song and dance acts which give the results of our Sin (though sin is unnamed. Horrors! You couldn't bring that word in here!). Gabrielle, Tony, and a third dancer, dressed up like baby triplets, sing a very realistic "Song of the Triplets," which soon becomes the rage in every drugstore and jukebox across the land:

> We do everything alike. . . .
> And what is more
> We hate each other very much,
> We hate our folks. . . .[1]

Etcetera, etcetera, etcetera!

The musical ends with a final song and dance routine portraying a murder mystery. The detective (Tony) declares in extended bars of rhythm, "Killers have to die." In the hot fluster of fear and passion he kills what he thinks is the criminal, but it turns out to be the woman he loves (Gaby). Thus the denouement—the criminal is inside of us and ends up by making us kill the one we love.

Shades of Paul and Ovid! "Wretched man. . . ! Who will deliver me from this body of death?"

How similar the verdict in the morality plays and dramas of the Middle Ages, except in these ancient plays and poetic epics the Sin is named and specified. The tragic results are the same horrible death in life as in the modern *Band Wagon*. It is interesting to note that in medieval poetry and drama the seven deadly sins are usually represented by animals. Medieval man thought of himself as a son of God with an eternal destiny, but striving with the animal in him. Modern man leaves out the idea of himself as a son of God and is content to be the animal. Look at the procession of the animals representing the sins in medieval literature: pride is variously represented as a lion, peacock, eagle, horse, or bull; envy as a dog, snake, wolf, dragon, boar, or toad; anger as a wolf, toad, pig, rat, rooster, dragon, or snake; avarice as a wolf, fox, hawk, elephant, ass, spider, or snake; sloth as an ass, a sow, or an ape; lechery most often as a goat, then as a pig, a snake, a dog, or a frog; and gluttony as a bear, a dog, a pig, or a wolf.[2]

Wrath with a Knife in His Mouth

Don't think this death in life belongs just to modern man, however. The morality plays and other drama of the Middle Ages draw the same picture, except that in them the Sin is named.

Spenser's *Faerie Queene*, in describing the procession of the sins as six "unequall beasts" driven by Lucifera, or Pride, places Wrath as the partner of Envy. "Fierce revenging Wrath" sits astride a lion and bears a "burning brond" in one hand and a knife in the other. Most of the figures representing wrath in this period are depicted with a knife, indicating the destructiveness of anger.

In an ancient painting by Peter Brueghel, done in 1558, Wrath is pictured with a knife in his mouth, a vial of poison in one hand

[2] See M. W. Bloomfield, *The Seven Deadly Sins* (East Lansing, Mich.: Michigan State College Press, 1952).

and the other hand in a sling, having been injured in previous battles, and sitting astride a barrel filled with fighting and dying men. Behind Wrath is a warrior's tent where a naked human body is being turned on a spit over the fire and a long-nosed helper is pouring a ladle of burning lead over the body, while the vultures outside pick the bones of other victims. In the foreground and background of the painting are processions of warriors in armor, with all kinds of murderous implements, trampling on their victims. Around the angry killers rise the flames of destruction.

Langland's *Piers Plowman* pictures "Wrathe" with his "nekke hangynge forward" as he pursues his intolerant and revengeful way, as if to say it is not the body but the head of man that gets him into trouble.

Marlowe's Faustus as Wrath at the behest of Beelzebub gives his name and disposition to Faust: "I am Wrath: I had neither father nor mother; I leapt out of a lion's mouth when I was scarce an hour old; and I have been running ever since up and down the world with this case of rapiers, pounding myself when I could get none to fight withal. I was born in hell, and look to it for some of you shall be my father!"

This narrative of wrath in medieval literature comes to a fitting end with the description by William Dunbar, whose vivid Scottish imagination pictures Ire in the *Dance of the Seven Deadly Sins* in hell:

> Then, Ire came in with sturt and strife,
> His hand was aye upon his knife,
>   He brandished like a bear.
>   Boasters, braggarts, and bargainers,
>   After him, passed into pairs,
>   All ready in feir of war.
> In jacks, and scrips, and bonnets of steel,
> Their legs were chained to the heel,
>   Forward was their affeir:
>   Some, upon others with brandes beft:
>   Some jagged others to the heft,
>   With knives, that sharp could shear.

Such realism puts the work of modern "realists" to shame. Who would dare to call these descriptions exaggerated in our age of concentration camps and human furnaces, of defenseless civilians ruthlessly slain, and of atomic and hydrogen bombs capable of wiping out whole cities?

The Dance of the Seven Deadly Sins—Modern Style

Some imaginative modern Dunbar might well describe the procession of the seven deadly sins in a twentieth-century hell. In such a description Pride might ride not in a chariot but in a Cadillac. Envy and Jealousy would still break up homes and tear souls to bits, but their cry could not be heard above the raucous laughter of a television comedy. Envy and Wrath, side by side in fiendish glee as pilot and bombadier in a jet bomber, dressed like diplomats rather than fliers, would roar out over the ocean with a load of H-bombs to be dropped on New York or London, Moscow or Shanghai. Avarice, Lust, and Gluttony would produce their same harvest of bestiality, disease, and suffering, but in chromium-plated dinettes, nylon-draped couches, and foam-rubber beds. Dejection would bring the same ancient despair and self-loathing, not in a royal palace where there are no modern conveniences but in a penthouse on Fifth Avenue where an all-electric kitchen and other labor-saving devices give more and more time for "this death" to do its work.

One of George Bernard Shaw's most disturbing plays, Man and Superman, comes close to being just such a modern picture of man's pride as a force of death rather than the force of life he boasts about. Part of the play is a dream in which the characters become inhabitants of hell for a while, where the Devil himself is called up and carries on a lively conversation about the follies of man on the earth. Don Juan and the Devil agree in their scorn that man's pride of reason has got him into most of his trouble, though Don Juan insists that man's mind was meant for something nobler, while the Devil rejoices that "all Man's reason has done for him is to make him beastlier than any beast." This is a good thing, declares the Devil, for "one splendid body is worth the brains of a hundred dyspeptic, flatulent philosophers." Ah, but brainless magnificence of the body has been tried; Don Juan comes back. He reminds the Devil that the megatherium and the ichthyosaurus paced the earth "with seven-league steps," but are only fossils in museums now. Though they wanted to live, they destroyed themselves from lack of intelligence in carrying out their purpose. The Devil rises triumphantly at this and points out that with all his "boasted brain" man is acting like the beasts and is destroying himself. "Have you walked up and down upon the earth lately?" he asks Don Juan. "I have; and I have examined Man's wonderful inventions," he continues.

And I tell you that in the arts of life man invents nothing; but in the arts of death he outdoes Nature herself, and produces by chemistry and machinery all the slaughter of plague, pestilence, and famine. The peasant I tempt today eats and drinks what was eaten and drunk by the peasants of ten thousand years ago; and the house he lives in has not altered as much in a thousand centuries as the fashion of a lady's bonnet in a score of weeks. But when he goes out to slay, he carries a marvel of mechanism that lets loose at the touch of his finger all the hidden molecular energies, and leaves the javelin, the arrow, the blowpipe of his fathers far behind. . . . There is nothing in Man's industrial machinery but his greed and sloth: his heart is in his weapons. This marvellous force of Life of which you boast is a force of Death: Man measures his strength by his destructiveness! [3]

Why is man a bungler, so that the arts of peace, the scientific advances that could be for his good, are producing death rather than life? The words of the Shavian devil are in this instance true wisdom; not because man lacks brains, but because "his heart is in his weapons." His major concern is for his own self-exaltation. He is more concerned with ways of venting his wrath than with ways of sharing the good of a heavenly Father's provision for all men.

In a modern portrait of wrath, therefore, the knife in the mouth of Ire would become a gun; the gun, too inadequate, would become

---

[3] Used by permission of The Public Trustee and The Society of Authors.

a 240-millimeter cannon; the artillery, too earth-bound, would change to a tank, then to a plane with blockbuster bombs; the blockbusters, too limited, would become an atomic bomb; and the A-bomb, soon child's play, would grow up into a hydrogen bomb; and the H-bomb —well from there it requires a truly Mephistophelian imagination to paint the rest. Man's heart is in his weapons—tools of modern Ire by which man, trying to be as God, is destroying his peace and life. What a fiendish dance of the seven deadly sins in the twentieth-century hell could be portrayed if only someone were truly imaginative! But "must a Christ perish in every generation to save men with no imagination?"

Blind Anger

It could be said of the intolerant, the wrathful, that they have no imagination. They are blind. Perhaps this is the reason men speak of blind anger. Anger presupposes pride, which is drawing a picture of myself and my position that is not according to reality, and falling down and worshiping it as my God. I cannot bear with, I am intolerant of, I am angry toward, any who fail to recognize my godliness or to fall down and worship me and do my bidding. Look at the blindness that cries, "I am the wise one—my ideas (or the ideas of my class, nation, or group) are ultimate."

"I know what is good—there couldn't be anything beyond what I think is important."

"We have the last word on all questions, a corner on the truth— everything wise begins and ends with us!"

Note that when man as an individual person feels defeated, his quickest reaction is to join some egoistic group in which he still tries to preserve his godlike superiority. And there is no intolerance, no wrath, no vengeance, so terrible as that of individual persons lost in a mob—whether you call it a party, a class, a race, a nation, or whatever. When the state becomes God, or the class or group takes the place of God, the result is mutiplied disaster. In our complex society it is easy to sin by syndicate and feel perfectly safe and honorable. The threats to man's very existence today are made possible by the individual's acquiescence to the infallible necessities of our group gods.

Demon Intolerance

On one of the quiet streets of a little American town there is to be seen a sign in front of a little church which says, "We are the only Church recognized by Jesus Christ." Such a spirit in a church calling itself Christian, though not as deadly, is similar to the intolerance of the Nazis, who assumed a ludicrous superiority over all mankind. Their brand of superman, with his know-it-all attitude, made them the most intolerant people on earth. Nothing was tolerated that disagreed with them or got in their way. Hence the justification for murdering over five million Jews and the imprisonment and torture of thousands of Christians who refused to accept the new myth of race and blood. The cruelty and beastliness were justified by the "righteousness of our cause." Their program was a "Wave of the Future"—a whole people trying to play God.

Now come the Communists to rule out God, not only in practice but in theory. A purge taking a hundred thousand lives, twenty thousand Greek children snatched from their homes, millions dying in slave labor camps—all of this is amply justified as a means to the establishment of a world where only one idea, one way, is permitted. Lenin, Stalin, Malenkov, and other mouthpieces of the Soviet Republics make clear that Communism and capitalism cannot exist side by side.

From the "Theses of the VI World Congress of the Communist International" in 1928 come these clear words:

The proletariat in the Soviet Union harbors no illusions as to the possibility of a durable peace with the imperialists. The proletariat knows that the imperialist attack against the Soviet Union is inevitable; that in the process of a proletarian world revolution, wars between proletarian and bourgeois states, wars for the emancipation of the world from capitalism, will necessarily and inevitably arise. Therefore, the primary duty of the proletariat, as the fighter for socialism, is to make all the necessary political, economic, and military preparations for these wars.[4]

Lenin's declaration in 1919 evidently has been the assumption ever since: "The existence of the Soviet Republic side by side with imperialist states for a long time is unthinkable. One or the other must triumph in the end. And before that end supervenes, a series of frightful collisions between the Soviet Republic and the bourgeois states will be inevitable."[5]

From such intolerance the "frightful collisions" threatening to spread to a world catastrophe do rather "inevitably" come. This is just another and more disastrous version of egoistic man trying to play God.

In every age the same brand of cruelty and injustice, though on a lesser scale, has been produced by religious bigots, such as the leaders of the Inquisition, who thought they possessed all the truth and tortured and killed any who differed with them.

What a deadly toll of heartache and tragedy the sin of pride, with its resulting anger and intolerance, has taken in the life of mankind!

It is easy, of course, to point out this sin in others; but what is needed first is to bring the truth closer home and see that whereever there are cruelty and injustice and unkindness in our own families and communities, between labor and industry, between different racial or religious groups, it is the result of the same sort of intolerance, on a lesser scale, as that of men and women who think they are the ultimate authority and are impatiently unwilling to brook opposition.

Most unresolved labor difficulties arise because management is intolerant of labor and labor of management. Each feels the ultimate right and good is on "our side." They refuse to find any third viewpoint in which peace and prosperity would be realized for everyone.

A parent who lacks the capacity to endure contradictions starts slapping and shouting at the children for the same basic reason that

---

[4] From *International Press Correspondence of the VI World Congress of the Communist International 1928*, Nov. 28, 1928.

[5] *Ibid. Report of Central Committee at 8th Party Congress* (1910).

a Nazi or a Communist goes berserk and starts beating or persecuting those who get in his way. Discipline for our children is necessary, but an angry, intolerant parent's discipline does more harm than good. The husband or wife who would be the all-wise, superior It must have his or her lordship recognized and accepted or be unbearable.

Impatience is another name for my inability to bear with those who deny or make light of my godlikeness. When I want my vision to succeed, regardless, any vindictiveness or cruelty is justified by the malice in my mind. I may be ashamed of my temper and of my unkind or even cruel acts, but after all the victim deserved it. What right did he have to call me a liar? Etcetera, etcetera, etcetera!

Hebble Tyson, mayor of the medieval town in Christopher Frye's play *The Lady's Not for Burning*, tries to exonerate himself from any blame in sentencing Jennet Jourdemayne to burn as a witch. She is an innocent young woman whose only crime is that she likes to live alone, to delve into her deceased father's alchemy, and that she has a peacock for a pet. The mayor says to Thomas, Jennet's only defender:

> Worthless creatures,
> Both; I call you clutter. The standard soul
> Must mercilessly be maintained. No
> Two ways of life. One God, one point of view.
> A general acquiescence to the mean.[6]

Hebble Tyson's lines are strangely contemporary. How great are the tragedies created every day by minds that insist on "one point of view. . . . No two ways of life. . . . A general acquiescence to the mean"—or else!

Such intolerance constantly feeds the fires of racial prejudice and hatred. Races who consider themselves superior are always intolerant of other races for the simple reason that the "Standard Soul" cannot be maintained if the inferior is allowed to get out of hand. They must be kept in their place. For instance, there are those who say, "I can't stand an uppish Negro." Of course an uppish white man is just as objectionable to an unprejudiced person. Nevertheless an intolerant white will easily tolerate an uppish white while going into a rage over an uppish Negro. Prejudice is the blindness of the person who is down on something he is not up on. Intolerance toward other races is always the result of insecurity which hides behind pride. Reinhold Niebuhr points out:

In the relations of majority and minority racial groups, for instance, the majority group justifies the disabilities which it imposes upon the minority group on the ground that the subject group is not capable of enjoying or profiting from the privileges of culture or civilization. Yet it can never completely hide, and it sometimes frankly expresses the fear that the grant of such privileges would eliminate the inequalities of endowment which supposedly justify the inequalities of privilege.[7]

Why Destruction?

Man desires peace, he says. Every government pronounces it solemnly. Every individual proclaims it. He does not want to fight, but he is forced into it. If only other people would recognize his rights, would do what he says, there could be peace in his home, his community, his world. Prophets of doom in foreboding passages such as the one quoted from Bernard Shaw tell of the possibility of destroying civilization and leaving in the world only a few scattered cave dwellers with geiger counters instead of typewriters. And individual men and women read and shrug their shoulders, and proceed to the next job with the knife. He cannot refrain from knifing his competitor in business who has discovered a better product. She cannot refrain from knifing the friend who walked off with the choice position in the club which, by rights, belonged to the one with the knife. Day after day he knifes the one he loves, or is supposed to love, most; and she knifes him in return. Wounds and suppurating sores take the place of healthy hearts, and proud flesh

[7] *Op. cit.* Used by permission of Charles Scribner's Sons.

takes the place of sweet flesh as God made it to be. He and she belong to the forces of death in the world rather than life.

Yes, man longs for peace, but not the things that make for peace. He wants to save himself from destruction, but not from the Sin which causes destruction. "After all, it is not right to let anybody run over you"—and in his endeavor to protect himself he is victim to blind anger and destructive intolerance.

Who can deliver him? Answer: Nobody, not even God, so long as he is hell-bent on saving this deceptively delightful ego-image which during the years he has built up within himself. The law declared by Jesus is as sure as the law of gravity: "Whoever would save his life will lose it."

How Could a God of Love Permit Such Loss?

The problem of evil in free men under the love of God is not something that can be tossed off with a few wise sentences and apt quotations, as some seem to think. It is too deep-seated within the mysteries of our being and the being of God to describe glibly. Only in humility at the foot of the cross where the Son of God was crucified and died rather than ask for his Father's cancelation of man's freedom, but prayed instead, "Father, forgive them. . ."—only here can any fitting word be said. This word points to the fact that *agape* in God is not a sickly sentiment which indulges his children when they try to take over the rein of creatorship and when they attempt to make others do their will. "No, the love of God is not the indulgence of a mother to a corrupt and wayward child. The love of God is the most exacting thing in the universe." He will not spoon-feed his favorites while others not knowing the magic formulas are destroyed. He is not a superego who delights in inflating our little egos; he is a wise Father, whose willingness to give to his children is greater than that of any earthly father, but who is unwilling to settle for anything less than that each of us should arrive to the "measure of the stature of the fullness of Christ" (Eph. 4:13).

It is for discipline that you have to endure. God is treating you as sons; for what son is there whom his father does not discipline? If you are left without discipline, . . . then you are illegitimate children and not sons. . . . Therefore lift your drooping hands and strengthen your weak knees, and make straight paths for your feet, so that what is lame may not be put out of joint but rather be healed. Strive for peace with all men, and for the holiness without which no one will see the Lord. (Heb. 12:7-8, 12-14.)

God's justice as seen in Christ, therefore, is a part of his love. We must suffer if we would learn the truth of our family relationship with God and our brothers and find his way to peace among men. God loves us too much to exempt any one of us from suffering. As the writer of Hebrews puts it, we may suffer either as sons, productively and with open heart, or we will suffer as illegitimate sons with increasing bitterness and loss.

There are two ways in which as sons we may suffer productively: (1) We may learn from the destructive pain meted out to us by others in their reaction to our attempt to dominate them. When we overreach our true position, the resistance we meet in others is the God-ordained justice to level us down to size. When we meet the destructive anger of our fellows with open mind and humble heart, asking, "In what way did my attitudes and acts properly bring this hostile reaction?" then we may learn some of life's choicest lessons. Much of our suffering, however, is unjustified by anything we have done. (2) We may learn from the vicarious pains which we receive as members of the human family, where the innocent are permitted to suffer with the guilty and because of the guilty. If God permits his beloved Son to suffer on the cross because of and for our sins in order to make peace between man and God, why, therefore, should I resent being called upon to suffer the wrongs done by other members of the divine family? By accepting my part of the pains of belonging to the family, I may grow in my own character as well as help redeem the guilty who cause my pains. Then I can help overcome evil with good and hate with love. This is the "holiness without which no one will see the Lord."

For if I refuse to suffer redemptively, I will suffer negatively as a prodigal son, a rebel in a far country, beating my head against the same wall of God's wise, loving resistance to the foolish quest of my self-image. I bump into this wall in the wrath of my fellows day after day, month after month, year after year, until I learn to respect the truth as it is and not as I want it to be, or until I have let my best possibilities be destroyed. Such is the costliness of our human freedom. We are free to choose among the kinds of suffering we will meet, but not free to choose a life free from all suffering. We may choose either the suffering of failure and death, or the redemptive suffering of growth and life. The second choice is salvation, for in it we share with Him "who for the joy that was set before him endured the cross, despising the shame" (Heb. 12:2), and is the revelation of the heart of God. Even God chooses to suffer, because he loves. This is the good news which makes peace and forgiveness possible.

The Children of God Are the Peacemakers

Why does the love of God for us and his willingness to suffer with us make peace and forgiveness possible? The answer to that question is one of the profoundest mysteries of the universe. Part of the answer lies deep in the nature of God himself, and we cannot fathom it. The most we can do is to accept the fact by faith that the suffering love of God does make peace and forgiveness possible, and that these words describing it are symbols of the blessed reality which is deep in the nature of God. Man has always groped for words to describe his spiritual relationships. The prophet Isaiah came closest to making words describe what the life and death of Jesus revealed when he portrayed God as saying:

> I, I am He
>   who blots out your transgressions for my own sake, . . .
> Fear not, O Jacob my servant, . . .
> I will pour my Spirit upon your descendants, . . .
> This one will say, "I am the Lord's," . . .
> Another will write on his hand, "The Lord's," . . .

> Fear not, for you will not be ashamed; . . .
> For your Maker is your husband,
>   the Lord of hosts is his name;
> and the Holy One of Israel is your Redeemer,
>   the God of the whole earth he is called.
> For the Lord has called you
>   like a wife forsaken and grieved in spirit. . . .
> with everlasting love I will have compassion. . . .
> For the mountains may depart
>   and the hills be removed,
> but my steadfast love shall not depart from you,
>   and my covenant of peace shall not be removed.
>   (Isa. 43:25; 44:2-3, 5; 54:4, 5-6, 8, 10.)

There is a mystery of divine love in whose own nature and being man is needed, so that on God's part there is a relationship established with his created children. Since we are finite, we can think of this relation only in human terms, such as that of a father with his son or a husband with his wife. God would forgive us for his own sake—"Your maker is your husband," says this tender foregleam of redemptive love. Though

> like a wife forsaken and grieved in spirit. . . .
> with everlasting love I will have compassion. . . .
> and my covenant of peace shall not be removed.

To some this noble conception is the height of man's egotism— to think that the mighty Maker has any need of our love! And it would be egotism to the nth degree were it not for one fact: the fact of Christ—the love that was revealed in the Spirit of Jesus and that has been the most powerful force on earth in the centuries since his death and resurrection. Here is the force of life and not death in human kind. If we are in the family relation to which the Spirit of Christ has brought us, we are able to say of a certainty, "I am the Lord's. I am not my own; I am bought with a price;

therefore I will glorify God in my body and in my life, which is God's." (See I Cor. 6:19-20.)

Dante's vision of Purgatory led him to the third terrace, where he saw those suffering from the sin of anger. Here to the accompaniment of the singing of the angelic choir, "Blessed they, the peacemakers: they know not evil wrath," Dante felt another sin mark erased; and he went forward with new hope.

And well he might, for here is the hope of the world, proclaimed by the first angelic choir announcing the birth of Jesus: "On earth peace among men with whom he is pleased!" Those who can say, "I am the Lord's," are the only ones who can keep through all sufferings and persecution the good will of *agape* love toward those who oppose and threaten them. They are the peacemakers, capable of practicing the mighty grace of magnanimity in a world of hate and strife.

The insight of Isaiah is also a foregleam of the axiom of modern clinical psychiatry that the mature person who is able to have affirmative love toward others is the one who is himself secure in love.

> O afflicted one, storm-tossed, and not comforted,
>   behold, I will set your stones in antimony,
>   and lay your foundations with sapphires.
>
> .   .   .   .
>
> In righteousness you shall be established.
>   (Isa. 54:11, 14.)

The figure of speech is understood by those who know that precious stones are the most secure and stable foundations possible for any working mechanism. The number and quality of jewels in a watch determine its dependableness. To those of us "afflicted . . . , storm-tossed, and not comforted," longing for assurances of love from others and of our own lovableness, the new relation with God, who freely forgives us and accounts us as worthy of his eternal love, will "lay [our] foundations with sapphires," so that we are able to live from a deep inner security. We, too, can love affirmatively and live magnanimously.

The Mighty Grace of Magnanimity

"Magnanimity" is a beautiful word which includes not only patience but the more active manifestations of love. It comes from two Latin words meaning "great-mindedness." To be possessed of strong convictions and yet willing to let other people have convictions that differ with and contradict mine; to be able to sustain danger and trouble with tranquillity and firmness, disdaining injustice and meanness; acting with a firm purpose in a noble cause—this is magnanimity. The sweet graces of magnanimity, of patient love in action! How precious in any time, but especially in our fear-torn, love-hungry, intolerant age!

We do not become peacemakers in our own strength, nor magnanimous by our own volition. The belief that we can has been the fatal mistake of many leading thinkers in Europe and America during the past century. John Dewey, who had a greater influence on American education than any other one man, and other writers and teachers such as Harry Overstreet, who contributed The Mature Mind, and similar books and articles have added largely to our understanding of the goal of education, but nonetheless have preached a "bootstrap religion." Be broadminded, be liberal, be generous, and teach your children to be kind, to possess affirmative love; for this liberal, mature, magnanimous mind is the hope of the world. Time has proved them right in the latter statement, but wrong in thinking that man can rid himself of his bigoted, selfish ideas. The widespread reversion to paganism in the nations where liberal humanism has been most exalted clinches this lesson. "If we are animals, why shouldn't we snarl?" makes more sense to the mass mind than the completely irrational teaching of the optimistic humanist who sings his seraphic vision, "Little children, you have sprung from the animals; you are basically nothing but an animal with an unusual forebrain; therefore let us love one another."

The angelic choir of eternal truth still sings, "Blessed are the children of God who can be magnanimous, for they are the peace-makers."

How Do We Become the Children of God?

How does your child become your child? A study in human relationships within the family affords the best parable of divine relationships in the family of God.

First, you want the child and by your own free will give birth to the child, or else you adopt a child not of your own blood. In any case the first requirement, if he is to be your child, is that you want him and let him know that he is wanted.

Second, as a response to this love which gave him birth and affirms his worth in every possible way, the child accepts his place in the family life as your child. For a while this acceptance of himself as belonging to you and to the home is unconscious. Then there comes a time when he makes it a matter of his own free choice. He has undergone the hurts of discipline, which have made him question your love and doubt his belonging; but through your forgiveness and steady manifestation of care and concern he decides against running away from home or remaining in the house all swelled-up with resentment and pride. Instead he accepts your forgiveness, trusts your good intentions, though he may not at all times understand them, and by his own choice becomes and remains your child.

Third, he learns that he cannot accept your love and keep the peace of belonging to the home unless he accepts his brothers and sisters in the same relationship. He becomes a peacemaker in the home when he most truly accepts his place in the home and is most secure in your love. He does not try to make peace with his brothers and sisters in order to buy your love, but rather because of your love and the sense of belonging, which are too priceless to be broken by continued quarreling and fighting.

Let us pursue this analogy in our relations with God and his family:

First, the initiative belongs to God; he *chose us* to be his children. This is the wonderful meaning of the doctrine of election in the Scriptures: *all* are chosen, not that some are chosen and some are not; "whosoever will, may come" (see Rev. 22:17). "God . . . sending his own Son in the likeness of sinful flesh" (Rom. 8:3) did what the law could not do—gave to us the assurance only dimly grasped by the prophets that God *wants us*. Because of his great love toward us, he gave his only Son. Our heavenly Father needs us, needs me. This is the unequaled security of any soul who truly understands the Christian gospel. "The Spirit himself bearing witness with our spirit that we are children of God." (Rom. 8:16.) Believe that and you will be secure.[8]

Second, I accept myself as belonging to God and to the blessed Family. This is my response to his love, which calls me to a dear belonging to him as his son and which assures me of my infinite worth to him. This is faith in the simplest, most elemental sense. Such faith may be taken for granted in my childhood days if I am brought up in a truly Christian home; but as soon as I feel the stirrings of prideful self-love with its envy, anger, resentment, and jealousy, and have been hurt by others and have hurt them, I begin to question his love and to rebel at his discipline. Then I may choose to run away from home like the prodigal son in open defiance of his love, trying to satisfy my soul on the husks of physical pleasure and material things. Or I may choose to remain at home like the elder brother, going through the forms of worship, dutifully working at being good while rebellious and proud in heart, boasting of my good deeds, my faithfulness, but still not being at home in my Father's house. Then through continued revelations of his love, the goodness that breaks in upon my isolated soul in countless ways, and some sudden confrontation of

> The heart that bled and broke to send
> God's love to earth's remotest part,

I see the folly of my ways. I come to myself, turn back to the

[8] See final chapter on deliverance from anxiety.

open arms of his forgiveness, willing to trust where I cannot see; and by my own choice I accept myself as his son.

Third, I learn that when I am out of harmony with any of my brothers and sisters in the human family, this faith is lost and my relationship is broken. I cannot be forgiven when I am unwilling to forgive. I cannot have communion with the eternal Father when my communion is broken by my own attitude with any of his children. It is in this context that Jesus said, "Love your enemies and pray for those who persecute you, so that you may be sons of your Father who is in heaven" (Matt. 5:44-45). That is to say, your dear belonging to the heavenly relationship is so priceless that you become a peacemaker because of it.

Much more needs to be understood to make the dramatic truths illustrated in this homely analogy live in our hearts with ever-increasing effectiveness. It seems pertinent in the conclusion of this particular chapter to add further word concerning the second and third conditions of our coming into the family of God as his willing, trusting, obedient children.

Love Yourself in Christ

This phrase is the equivalent of "accept yourself as God's son"; for when we are in the spirit of Christ, or in Christ, we do affirm ourselves in the true meaning of *agape*. We love God's purposes for us and believe in our own worth as God believes in it.

This loving oneself in the perspective of reality cuts the root of much anger and irritation, envy and hate, which in the final analysis are evidences of our self-disgust as well as our self-exaltation. While these symptoms are more in the category of the sin of accidie, or dejection, which will be treated more fully in the following chapter, it is necessary to deal briefly with this reverse side of self-exaltation here in order to understand the conflict within ourselves which leads to conflict with others. If there is a war within us, there will be war outside of us. "The worst disease of human life is self-hate and self-loathing." Here we must agree with Nietzsche and Fromm. Sometimes when one stubs his toe on a chair, he kicks the chair, or wants to kick it, because it got in his way. The chair in his way is a symbol of his inner frustration. When we are seeking false goals and are unable to reach them, we feel like kicking ourselves; and we end up by hating the self we sought to exalt. It is only when we accept God's infinite goal for us, much of which we cannot yet see, and become the persons which in Christ we see we were meant to be that we are able to love ourselves affirmatively and joyously, and at the same time love others, even those who get in our way.

Sergius, the young army-officer hero in Bernard Shaw's *Arms and the Man*, has hurled himself passionately into the quest of becoming first a hero and then an exalted lover, only to find himself betrayed by his baser self. He has been making love to Louka, his fiancee's maid, who tells him that his fiancee, Raina, has been untrue to him. With a bluster of arrogance he commands Louka to remember that a "gentleman does not discuss the conduct of the lady he is engaged to with her maid." Whereupon Louka gives him a stinging rebuke: "It's so hard to know what a gentleman considers right," she cries. "I thought from your trying to kiss me that you had given up being so particular. . . . I expect one of the six of you is very like me, sir." She was referring to his former statement about being six different Sergiuses.

Striking his forehead, Sergius says bitterly to himself, "Which of the six is the real man? thats the question that torments me. One of them is a hero, another a buffoon, another a humbug, another perhaps a bit of a blackguard"; and he adds as he looks with traces of shame at Louka, "And one, at least, is a coward: jealous, like all cowards!" [9]

When we are filled with the conflict of the six of us fighting for the mastery, and the only judge of them is the ego-vision thus torn apart, we cannot truly love ourselves.

> From much perplexing care I would be free,
> If I could once determine which is Me!

[9] Used by permission of The Public Trustee and The Society of Authors.

No man can be patient and tolerant with others who is impatient and intolerant with himself. How great is the freedom of one "to whom the Eternal Word speaketh; he is delivered from a multitude of opinions," says the profound Christian thinker in the *Imitation of Christ*.

He to whom all things are one, who reduceth all things to one, and seeth all things in one, may enjoy a quiet mind and remain peaceable in God [and with his brethren]. Who hath harder combat than he that laboureth to overcome himself? . . . If I be left to myself, behold! I become nothing, but mere weakness; but if Thou for an instant look upon me, I am forthwith made strong and filled with new joy. And a great marvel it is, that I am so suddenly lifted up, and so graciously embraced by Thee, who of my own weight am always sinking downward. Thy love is the cause hereof. . . . For indeed by loving myself amiss, I lost myself; and by seeking Thee alone, and purely loving Thee, I have found both myself and Thee, [and thus I have found my neighbor].

To love myself in Christ is the prelude to loving my neighbor in Christ; the one is impossible without the other.

Killed by Kindness

This, then, is the portrait of one who belongs to the family of God and has found—or maybe I should say, is finding—himself in a quiet, peaceful, trusting love. He is able to love his enemies, to rejoice when he is persecuted, to turn the other cheek, to go the second mile. He becomes not a doormat over which others walk, but a door through which they too may enter and possess the positive peace of conflicts resolved, sins forgiven, and life made new. Criticism, persecution, opposition, are agape love's best opportunity. Free on the inside of bitter frustrations, one can seek to free others about him from the frustrations that cause them to strike out in blind rage at him and at others. This, said Jesus, is the blessed spirit of those who belong to the family of God. They are able to live by the Golden Rule and to do something positive in return for blows and slights and persecutions, such as carrying the soldier's pack not only the one mile required by law, but two miles as an opportunity to reveal their good will; or turning the other cheek while saying, in effect, "Friend, why art thou hurting thyself; let me help thee from thy sickness to the health which is the gift of God." (See Matt. 5:38-41.) It is not the turning of the cheek that is important, but the turning of wrath into a consciousness of being loved and forgiven.

Walter M. Horton tells the story of a pious deacon who "goaded apparently beyond endurance by the persistent malice of an enemy, publicly vowed to 'kill him.' The enemy heard of his vow and laughed to his friend over what the 'good, harmless old fool would do.'" What the deacon did, to the astonishment of everyone, was to take every opportunity to do his enemy good. At first it was a source of merriment and then of annoyance; but in the end, after the deacon had risked his life in saving the man's wife from drowning, "the deadlock between the two was broken and a new relationship set up. 'All right,' said the man, 'You've done what you said you'd do, and I admit it. You've killed me—or at least you've killed the man that I was. Now, what can I do for you?'" [10]

It should be noted that agape love is not always successful in turning away the wrath of the enemy. If so, there would be no Cross. To consider love as the chief weapon to make people do what is right whether they want to or not is to twist agape into eros. Neither do we decide to use agape love merely in order to save ourselves and civilization. True, the cessation of war and other blessings would be the result if enough of mankind loved one another as brothers in the family of God; nevertheless the saving of ourselves and our civilization is not the deepest motive.

Why then should we desire to love our enemies? Why want to kill their false selves by kindness? Because this is God's way with us. He, too, has sought to kill our false misplaced self-love, to deliver us from our Sin, that he might bring us into the "glorious liberty of the children of God" (Rom. 8:21). We love him because

[10] *Our Christian Faith* (Boston: Pilgrim Press, 1947).

he first loved us. Little children, if God so loved us, we ought also to love one another. This is the deepest motive from which *agape* love springs. We are not merely animals, snarling at one another, biting and devouring one another. We do not choose to go the way of the dinosaur and the ichthyosaurus to destruction, but the way of the redeemed sons and daughters of God in whom the love of God is perfected.

Blessed are those who have accepted their sonship with God. They are the merciful, magnanimous, patient peacemakers.

Chapter V

DEJECTION

Into Vital Concern—Love That Lifts

"You CANNOT IMAGINE HOW HORRIBLY I . . . BORE MYSELF," CRIED Hedda Gabler in Ibsen's play. How frequently such a confession describes much of our lives!

"I just don't give a hang." "So what?" "Oh, yeah!" "Aw, what the heck!" Or maybe you used stronger language. These American slang expressions describe the first minor manifestations of the sin of dejection or sloth. The equivalent phrase used by our British cousins when confronted by a great task, a big job needing to be done, or just the usual business of living is "Well, really, I couldn't care less!" as they, like us, throw up their hands in a gesture of utter indifference.

Here is the symptom of an ancient sin as old as man. It was well known in the Middle Ages, though it has been dropped from most modern categories of sin. Nevertheless it is still one of the costliest of the deadly sins, as modern as the latest show on television. Boredom is one of the least of its results. The pessimism, cynicism, and the deep sense of futility cutting the roots of vital concern in so many good-intentioned folk is the major devastation the sin of dejection leaves in its wake. It makes life really not worth living and prevents the creative action necessary to produce homes and communities and a world desirable to live in. "Hope springs eternal in the human breast" until we succumb to the final inroads of this sin.

True, some unusually discouraging events have transpired within the last quarter century. Man's hopes for peace in this generation have been pretty well snuffed out by world wars and their horrendous threats to make a shambles of the whole world. In the grip of gigantic forces beyond our control, it is comparatively easy for any individual to throw up his hands and ask, "Does what I do make any difference?" The prevailing answer of current pessimists is, "No, of course not. Human nature cannot be changed. From man's greed and selfishness, his pride and envy, his brutality and hate, you cannot expect anything more than an increase in tensions and conflicts." These evils have always existed in humanity, but man has not always had atomic bombs and jet planes with which to vent his wrath and show his power. Of course civilization is doomed! cry these cynics. What more could you expect, scorns Haeckel, for "man is nothing but a vertical vertabrae with a perfect sewage system." Another mutters about human life being nothing but "organic scum on one of the meanest planets . . . the disease of aglutinated dust." Bertrand Russell wails about the "slow, sure doom" that is falling on man, "pitiless, and dark." He counsels, as did the ancient Stoics, that the best thing for man to do is to build as firmly as possible on the "foundations of unyielding despair."

Despair

But what kind of life is it that can be built upon such foundations? Nothing noble and enduring, of course; nothing with any lilt or joy or hopefulness or anticipation in it. Only dead, dull, bored, meaningless life—if it can be called life. We cannot escape feeling that Paul's description of "this death" fits many of us and our emptiness better than the word "life."

William Saroyan's satirical play *The Time of Your Life* pictures Joe, a bored young loafer with money and a good heart, trying to answer the question asked by a young lady in a waterfront saloon:

"Do you really *like* to drink?" she asks him.

"As much as I like to *breathe*," Joe answers.

"Why?" asks Mary.

And Joe speaks as though working out a problem: "Now, why do I drink? No. Why does anybody drink?"—and he works it out:

> Every day has twenty-four hours. . . . Out of the twenty-four hours at *least* twenty-three and a half are—my God, I don't know why—dull, dead, boring, empty, and murderous. Minutes on the clock, *not time of living* . . . [but] spent in waiting. . . . And the more you wait, the less there is to wait for. . . . That goes on for days and days and weeks and months and years, and years, and the first thing you know *all* the years are dead. All the minutes are dead. You yourself are dead.[1]

Why such death? Because we are waiting, waiting, waiting, for the dream ship of our ego-image to come in; and it never quite does. As a matter of fact, the opposite comes: failure, failure, failure. And as private souls trying to play God—or as a corporate soul elevating man's reason, or science, or Communism, or democracy, or America, or Britain, or any other group idea into the place of God—we simply cannot stand failure. As a matter of fact, all this pessimism, fatalism, and defeatism that sit astride our hopes and beliefs like a giant octopus are nothing in the world but the reverse English to the old song of the Enlightenment, "Glory to Man in the highest! for Man is the master of things," and of himself and of the whole universe. Just as hate is the underside of *eros* love, so despair and cynicism are always the underside of pride, which is also a manifestation of misplaced love.

The Latin word *accidia* is the name given by the early and medieval Christians to the despair and dejection resulting from the parent Sin. The word *accidia* has an interesting derivation, an understanding of which will be helpful in describing this sin. The word is derived from the Greek *akēdia*, which means literally "not caring" (a: not, plus *kidos*: care). When one fails often enough in achieving his self-made goals, he begins to be discouraged, then

[1] Used by permission of Harcourt, Brace & Co., Inc.

frustrated, then in despair, until he just doesn't give a hang. He simply doesn't care. He doesn't care what happens to others. He is callous and unconcerned over their suffering. He finally gets to the place where he doesn't care much about what happens to him. From the sin of dejection—the reverse of pride—come other sins, such as drunkenness, which Saroyan's Joe was using to cover up and escape his boredom. The sins of avarice, lust, and gluttony spring as often from the sin of dejection as from the sin of pride—the one seeking to debase, punish, and escape from oneself, and the other seeking to exalt, preen, and glorify oneself.

The outer manifestations of *accidia* are of two principal kinds: on one hand, dejection—lowness of spirits, depression,[2] the blues, boredom, ennui, leading finally to despair—on the other hand, sloth—laziness, slowness, sleepiness. No clear distinction can be made between sloth and dejection, for both arise from the deeper inner feeling of apathy and unconcern that forms one of the manifestations of the Sin of misplaced self-love.

My Gyntian Self

"A spark disturbs our clod," says Browning. But when this spark of divine discontent is misspent in exalting ourselves, in the hopeless quest to realize the image of our vision toward our own private version of superman, the inevitable result is increasing failure, unproductiveness, impotence. This, as I have said, we cannot stand; because it indicates we are not God and cannot build a world according to our own private specifications. *Accidia* is always one of the results of attempting to save and perpetuate what Ibsen's *Peer Gynt* calls his "Gyntian Self." The theme of the play indicates Peer Gynt's belief that through the devotion of his whole life to the interests of self he will become a great and successful person. It is well to note that the reason great drama is so effective is that it speaks what is unspoken within us. It reveals our selves inside and out, in action or in escape, better than any other medium.

[2] Not all depression of spirit is a symptom of sin. It may be due to physical exhaustion or illness, though even here there may be a close connection.

Let us, therefore, salute the Gyntian Self, which in some degree is in every one of us:

> The Gyntian Self!
> An army, that, of wishes, appetites, desires!
> The Gyntian Self!
> It is a sea of fancies, claims and aspirations;
> In fact, it's all that swells within my breast
> And makes it come about that I am I and live as such.[3]

This is Peer Gynt's belief in Scene I as the play begins; but as scene follows scene, progressive failures dog his steps. Even when he has success, rides in a yacht, travels widely, enjoys the best of food and music, he is a failure within and knows it. At the end he realizes that he has followed, not the true interests of his real self, but the false chimera of the Gyntian Self in which his true self has been lost. His unspoken goal was, in the words of the Trolls, "Be enough to thyself." Now he realizes how completely he has denied himself, as his unrealized possibilities come to taunt him of his Sin and to point the reason for his lack of productiveness:

> *The Threadballs*
> We are thoughts;
> You should have thought us;
> Little feet, to life
> You should have brought us!
> We should have risen
> With glorious sound;
> But here like threadballs
> We are earthbound.

> *Withered Leaves*
> We are a watchword;
> You should have used us!
> Life by your sloth
> Has been refused us.

[3] Used by permission of Random House.

Dejection

By worms we're eaten
All up and down;
No fruits will have us
For spreading crown.

A Sighing in the Air

We are songs:
You should have sung us!
In the depths of your heart
Despair has wrung us!
We lay and waited;
You called us not.
May your throat and voice
With poison rot!

Dewdrops

We are tears
Which were never shed.
The cutting ice
Which all hearts dread
We could have melted;
But now its dart
Is frozen into
A stubborn heart.
The wound is closed;
Our power is lost.

Broken Straws

We are deeds
You left us undone;
Strangled by doubt,
Spoiled ere begun.
At the Judgment Day
We shall be there
To tell our tale
How will you fare? [4]

[4] *Ibid.*

This is the despair of every Gyntian Self: strive as hard as he may, he always leaves something out; he misses the best; he flubs the highest—the "threadballs" of thoughts he should have thought and true heights he missed thereby; the withered leaves of faith in some true goal or watchword, unused, and the "fruits . . . for spreading crown" he then could not have; a "sighing in the air" of songs he should have sung that ended instead in the "poison rot" of despair; "dewdrops" of compassionate tears he never shed that could have cut the "ice which all hearts dread," but he left his own and theirs frozen by stubbornness, the wound closed, his power lost; and the "broken straws" of deeds left undone or "strangled by doubt" and "spoiled ere begun" which continually rise to haunt him. Every day is Judgment Day for one who seeks to save his Gyntian Self, only the sound of doom gets louder as age increases and the end draws near.

This Miserable Fate

There is a base inaction which is every bit as harmful and destructive as any action. This is the sin of dejection and sloth: the things we should have done that we have left undone, the coming short of the glory of God, missing the true goal of becoming sons of God and the joys of sharing in the fellowship of his family.

> Of all sad words of tongue or pen,
> The saddest are these: "It might have been!"

Dante in his vision of Hell, having just entered the gates over which were written the words "All hope abandon, ye who enter here" and hearing words of despondency and tones of wrath and weeping, cried, "O master! what is this I hear?" And his guide said to him:

> This miserable fate
> Suffer the wretched souls of those, who lived
> Without or praise or blame, with that ill band
> Of angels mix'd, who nor rebellious proved.

These had not rebelled at God, "nor yet were true to God."

114

From his bounds Heaven drove them forth
Not to impair his lustre; nor the depth
Of Hell receives them, lest the accursed tribe
Should glory thence with exultation vain.

.   .   .   .

These of death
No hope may entertain: and their blind life
So meanly passes, that all other lots
They envy. . . . Mercy and Justice scorn them both.
Speak not of them, but look, and pass them by.

Surely such a state of frustration and despair could never come to *me!* Thus the pride of Superman speaks. "Man is something that must be surpassed." "Go to, now, and overcome your boredom and apathy, build me 'Superman.' Do not await any redemption except *my* redemption. . . . Redeem the past and every 'It was' to transform it until the Will saith: 'But so did I will it! So shall it be, and so it is!' " [5]

The only catch is that man can never surpass himself. This is the judgment of God on man's finitude; therefore no matter how many years his life should be lengthened, he could never redeem the past, change the "it was" into what should be.

The Moving Finger writes; and, having writ,
Moves on: nor all your Piety nor Wit
Shall lure it back to cancel half a Line.

Enter guilt, which added to our failures increases despair; and the Gyntian Self can do absolutely nothing to remove it. Man simply cannot forgive himself, in the deepest sense, of his failures to live up to the false and exalted goals which he sets for himself; therefore the inevitable result of his Sin is self-condemnation, lead-

---

[5] From *Thus Spake Zarathustra* by Friedrich Nietzsche. Everyman's Library. Published by E. P. Dutton & Co., Inc. Used by permission of J. M. Dent & Sons, Ltd.

ing to self-distrust, then self-despair, then self-loathing. This is the hell to which even in this life the Gyntian Self leads. The ultimate end of pride is dejection, and the end of dejection is death. Such wages are collected regularly with interest.

Ways Out of Wits' End

Suicide is one way of attempting to escape "this death." When James V. Forrestal, former Secretary of Defense, jumped out of a high hospital window, he left by his bedside a book of Greek poetry opened at the "Chorus from Ajax" from Sophocles' dramatic study of insanity and suicide *Ajax*, with these words:

> When Reason's day
> Sets rayless—joyless—quenched in cold decay
> Better to die, and sleep
> The never-waking sleep, than linger on,
> And dare to live, when the soul's life is gone.

Dejection is the beginning of sunset for reason exalted to the place of God. The twilight is upon many who still strive to keep a stiff upper lip, and the cold chill of uncaring despondency is numbing the heart of any vital effort.

I read a letter from a man of the age to have served in World War II and to have received training in modern nihilism in his university days. He had given up all the old "superstitions" and accepted the pragmatist's universe, which has no fixed truth, "where right and wrong swirl through time and space, always dependent on local interpretation and individual desire," with ideals that must be forever "tested by individual experience and subject to change without notice." This young man tried first one ideal then another, including Communism, only to suffer a worse disillusionment, followed by years of wasted dissipation. *Accidia* had him in its grip, and life was being lost at a frightful clip. Then one day he turned from his self-loathing and self-hating ways to seek for the meaning of the old faith he had so scornfully rejected. He began to find a way out of Wits' End in a new faith in God as revealed in Christ. Writing to one of his former teachers, who had tried vainly in his high-school days to help him find such a faith, he said, "The thing which almost makes me weep at times is that almost every person I've ever known gives the impression that he has been sold out."

This sense of betrayal pervades the atmosphere in most circles of disappointed supermen; but too often the victims claim to be sold out by their enemies, or by the government, or by their teachers, or even by the Church and the leaders of religion. And it is indeed true that responsibility for building up the false hopes of the Gyntian Self rests not only on the individual but on the society in which he lives; and part of the blame rests on our homes, our schools, and even our churches.

Sold Out!

Although we are sold out in the final analysis, not by what others do, but by the acceptance of a misplaced love of self as our God, nevertheless the naïveté with which we betray our own best selves is accentuated by the influence of other self-loving victims about us. The self-righteous "Christians" who regard themselves as near saints, or at least as very good people, obscure for us the only way out of the debacle in which we will soon find ourselves. And the strutting would-be supermen about us, boasting of their ability to seize life by the forelock and make it what they want it to be, are so attractive to our youthful pride. Such influences lead us to follow the tantalizing but elusive dreams of our own making and thus to lose our one great hope of becoming a new creature in Christ.

However, following the behests of the Gyntian Self is our choice in the end—our Procrustean bed, and we have to lie on it. Since it is our own choice, we try to dress it up and make it look as good as we can. Hence the self-deception we practice as long as we can. We think more highly of ourselves than we ought to think because we have not seen what we really are. We cannot see the true picture of ourselves because of what psychologists call "rationalization"—the use of unconscious means of justifying and exalting ourselves in order to keep confidence in ourselves. Thus there is a basic dishonesty in all of us that is the necessary concomitant of self-love. "Man loves himself inordinately. Since his determinate existence does not deserve the devotion lavished upon it, it is obviously necessary to practice some deception in order to justify such excessive devotion." [6] This does not imply conscious dishonesty. The primary purpose of our rationalization is to deceive not others but ourselves. In order to keep up the little world of self that we have built, we practice self-deception; as Tertullian said, "The self contrives to prolong a willing ignorance and bribes knowledge to play a dishonest part."

One reason "it is easier for a camel to go through the eye of a needle than for a rich man to enter the kingdom of God" (Matt. 19:24) is the fact that one's self-deception may be greatly strengthened and encouraged by plenty of money or by a few years of worldly success. It is remarkable how a good bank account and a few luxuries can butter up our ego, so to speak, glossing over our failures and keeping us from seeing how unworthy we really are. But sooner or later all our blandishments and ego props fail; we are sold out.

Psalm 107 aptly describes the condition of our spirits when we are the victims of *accidia* and the reasons for being thus victimized:

> Some wandered in desert wastes. . . .
> Some sat in darkness and in gloom,
>   prisoners in affliction and in irons,
> for they had rebelled against the words of God,
>   and spurned the counsel of the Most High.
> Their hearts were bowed down with hard labor;
>   They fell down, with none to help.

Then follows the description of some ancient sailors as their ship was being tossed in a storm:

[6] Niebuhr, *op. cit.* Used by permission of Charles Scribner's Sons.

They mounted up to heaven, they went down to the depths;
    their courage melted away in their evil plight;
they reeled and staggered like drunken men,
    and were at their wits' end.

This Wits' End, which is becoming personally and collectively more familiar, is no modern invention. It belonged not only to these ancient sailors but to voyagers on the Sea of Life in every age. Medieval drama and poetry had a name for it. In numerous plays and epics the slothful man is portrayed as an ass, the antithesis of wit and smartness. In Spenser's *Faerie Queene* the lead animal in the procession of the sins driven by the whip of Pride is an ass, ridden by Idleness, the "nourse of sin," dressed in "Monkis garments," drowned in sleep, wracked by fever, with a little-used breviary in his hand.

The sin that leads us to Wits' End is truly the "nourse" (nurse) of other sins. Avarice, lust, gluttony, and drunkenness are only attempts to escape our inner failure. Here is Dunbar's description of it in the dance of the seven sins in hell:

> Sloth that at the second bidding
> Came like a sow out of a midden,
>   Full sleepy was his face.
>   Many a lazy stupid glutton,
>   And slattern daw and sleepy sloven,
>   Him served aye with sounyie.
>   He drew them forth in till a chain,
> And Belial with a bridle rein,
>   Ever lashed them on. . . .
> Then, Lechery, that loathly corse,
> Came neighing like a bagit horse;
>   And Idleness did him lead.

T. S. Eliot has drawn a modern picture of dejection and sloth in the cryptic poem "The Hollow Men":

We are the hollow men
We are the stuffed men
Leaning together
Headpiece filled with straw. Alas!
Our dried voices, when
We whisper together
Are quiet and meaningless
As wind in dry grass
Or rat's feet over broken glass
In our dry cellar.

.   .   .   .

    not as lost
Violent souls, but only
As the hollow men
The stuffed men.

.   .   .   .

This is the way the world ends
This is the way the world ends
This is the way the world ends
Not with a bang but a whimper.[7]

"Headpiece filled with straw" instead of wisdom—this is indeed the sad denouement of man who goes forth to conquer the world by his own bright reason and cannot even conquer himself. He is a hollow man, stuffed with things and sensations and discontented miseries instead of being filled with riches of joy and contentment. He who goes out to conquer the world by the might of his own hand finds the end of his world upon him, "not with a bang but a whimper."

This "miserable fate" is so disgusting and loathsome we feel like saying with Dante's guide at the gates of Hell, as they witnessed the victims of apathy and indifference, "Speak not of them, but look, and pass them by." This we cannot do, for in so many of us are found at least the seeds of dejection and bored unconcern. The sooner we realize that we can never become our Gyntian Selves

[7] *Collected Poems*. Used by permission of Random House.

and that it would be the greatest curse if we could, the sooner we will get around to the denial of our favorite methods of self-deception and rationalization by which we stave off the crisis a little longer. When we are able to admit our Sin as well as our sins, to recognize our guilt and utter inability to lift ourselves by the bootstraps into a life of *agape* love with its steadfast encouragement and vital concern, then we will be ready to recognize and admit the Deliverer. What a blessed moment when I cry at last, "Wretched man that I am! who will deliver me from this . . . death?" Then I will be ready to be delivered by the loving forgiveness of the God of encouragement and hope.

Why is it we cannot deliver ourselves from dejection and despair? Why cannot we transform our boredom and apathy into a vital concern? Because of two problems which we can never solve so long as we neglect or refuse to live in right relations with the loving Spirit of the God of steadfastness, encouragement, and hope who is revealed in Christ: namely, the problem of guilt and the problem of insignificance and meaninglessness.

The Problem of Guilt

"Guilt is the gap between the *ought* and the *is*," [8] and as finite, limited creatures we can never fill in the gap. "Guilt implies that one is held accountable by himself or by others for doing or feeling what was forbidden, or failing to do or feel what is required. [9] Guilt is usually accompanied by hostility and is the root of self-distrust and despair.

There is a certain kind of self-condemnation and self-distrust which is at the very heart of all healthy living. One supreme good in human experience is the ability to condemn ourselves when we have failed and been unworthy, and to feel guilty until we do something about it. Guilt, like pain, has a place in human life. Without pain one might keep his hand in the fire until it was burned to a

[8] James A. Pike, *Beyond Anxiety* (New York: Chas. Scribner's Sons, 1953).
[9] Sherrill, *op. cit.* Used by permission of John Knox Press.

crisp. Pain is nature's warning: "Take your hand out of the fire." Without guilt man might live in a fool's paradise, deceiving himself and others, until there was no hope for him to grow and improve. There is a healthy sense of guilt which is the beginning of all human advance.

This is true in spite of the contention of some psychiatrists that guilt is an unmixed evil. In order to get rid of it, they would banish sin to the limbo of all superstitious ideas. Your sense of guilt is false; recognize it, they say, and you are free. They would turn everybody into "nice" folk, as contrasted with "nasty" people who are always acknowledging their sins. "Nice" people are smug and complacent, "healthy" because they just don't have any sins or anything to feel guilty about.

Such unrealism is part of the reason the sin of dejection has such a grip on so many people today. These "liberated" moderns are not supposed to have any guilt. There are none but themselves to hold them accountable for what they are and do; therefore they are not guilty. But the unconscious mind does not accept the verdict of the conscious mind. Bitter self-condemnation and unrecognized guilt continue to work havoc in increasing depression, boredom, and self-loathing, which make them disgusted with life in general and everyone around them in particular.

Eugene O'Neill, who more than any other one writer helped American drama to come of age by portraying the deep inner conflicts of his characters, makes this inability to rid ourselves of guilt the central theme of one of his most provocative plays, *The Iceman Cometh.* Hickey, the drunken salesman in this sordid drama, the characters of which are all alcoholic bums, describes the loving way his wife forgave him time and again when he returned home after a spree, with a hang-over and even with evidences of his infidelity. Her love would conquer her disgust, and she would kiss him.

"Can you imagine what a guilty skunk she made me feel?" he asked his once-admiring companions who now were aghast as they heard him confess to murdering his wife.

Dejection

Can you picture all I made her suffer, and all the guilt she made me feel, and how I hated myself! . . . I even caught myself hating her for making me hate myself so much. There's a limit to the guilt you can feel and the forgiveness and pity you can take! You have to begin blaming someone else, too. I got so sometimes when she'd kiss me it was like she did it on purpose to humiliate me, as if she'd spit in my face! But all the time I saw how crazy and rotten of me that was, and it made me hate myself all the more. You'd never believe I could hate so much, a good-natured, happy-go-lucky slob like me! [10]

This is a law of life: unrelieved guilt always produces self-hate, and even the forgiving love of another person may not remove our guilt and self-loathing.

The experience of the race has upheld the viewpoint of Jesus. There is a godly sorrow that leads us to repentance and to a new life. Such self-condemnation is priceless indeed. The first requirement for healthy living is a deep sense of need and personal inadequacy that brings us to God and a fresh beginning each day. All great souls have had that kind of spirit. It wasn't a murderer or a thief who said, "I am the foremost of sinners" (I Tim. 1:15). It was the apostle Paul. It was Simon, the big-hearted fisherman just beginning to be the strong apostle Peter, who said, as he first stood in the presence of Jesus, "Depart from me, for I am a sinful man, O Lord" (Luke 5:8).

It is said of John Wesley that he felt the distance between himself and God, between himself and what he ought to be, as much as any person who ever lived. This kind of healthy self-condemnation is what we need. It is the unresolved guilt of would-be supermen which produces the despair and futility that throttle even their own good intentions and cut the root of their best efforts. This guilt cannot be laughed away or dismissed by any amount of knowledge.

Shakespeare said:

Our doubts are traitors,

[10] Used by permission of Random House.

123

And make us lose the good we oft might win
By fearing to attempt.

It is the inner distrust of one's ability to find meaning, joy, and victory in life which is most vicious and costly. Instead of letting our inadequacy lead us to the acceptance of our creaturehood and dependence on God, we cling to our self-love and try to hide our sense of inner failure. As was indicated earlier in the chapter, a great many of the escapist habits of man are the result of this attempt. For millions of Joes and Hickeys alcoholism is an attempt to escape from boredom and the plaguing sense of inner failure. One may try to drown oneself in noise, in a crowd, in a round of excitement, so that he does not hear the harsh voice of conscience scorned. It is obvious that if he refuses to face his failure, he will also be unable to recognize the sweet, encouraging voice of the Holy Spirit revealing the way out of his failure.

It is possible for anyone to protect himself for a while from this warning, helping, strengthening Voice. With average good fortune in our self-loving pursuits, we may get by rather well for several years. Then the age of forty arrives, or some other age when we expected to be most successful; and for many there is a crisis for the simple reason that self-condemnation begins to lift its ugly head in spite of the usual escape methods. We have been able so far to cover up our inability to find life and to do the things we really want to do most; but regardless of the appearance of success, we haven't achieved what deep down inside we had pictured. Life is slipping through our fingers, so we think we will be forgiven for taking one last splurge. The result (for example) is that grandpa or grandma takes one last fling. How many evil and foolish things people do in their attempts to escape from guilt and self-condemnation!

"There Is Therefore Now No Condemnation . . ."

These are truly the most beautiful words ever spoken or written, either in the Bible or in any other literature. They are the open sesame to a steadfast hope and never-failing encouragement. They are words of an eternal love in which I find myself forgiven, accepted —unworthy and failing as I am—loved and trusted by the Christ-like Father who is the God of all the universe, who wants my freedom and devoted trust more than any earthly father wants the freedom and devotion of his son. These are singing words that unloose all the pent-up hopelessness and frustration, and change the minor chords of wailing despair to major chords of deliverance. Such is the symphony of hope and love behind the apostle Paul's declaration: "There is therefore now no condemnation for those who are in Christ Jesus" (Rom. 8:1). For this was his experience, his description of his deliverance from the old man of misplaced self-love with its law of sin and death, its impossible goals, and its ineradicable guilt.

Forgiveness for Paul was the doorway into the new life in Christ Jesus, where to be in Christ is not only the hope of glory, but the experience of that glory in awesome measure for one poor human heart to bear. The fruit of the Spirit is Joy, and Hope, Peace, and Victory, all spelled with a capital because they are not the peace which the world gives (see John 14:27), not the poor deluded hopes or pipe dreams that tantalize us and leave us stranded, not the weak victory of man's ego passion which leaves us defeated and heartsick, and certainly not the temporary joy which comes from the satisfaction of our Gyntian Selves that soon leaves us joyless and loveless and lifeless. They are the Joy and Peace, the Hope and Victory, which the Lord of heaven and earth gives to his penitent and trusting children. "In [his] presence there is fullness of joy." (Ps. 16:11.) No wonder Paul was inspired to coin two new names for God as he prayed for the Christians in Rome:

May the God of steadfastness and encouragement grant you to live in such harmony with one another, in accord with Christ Jesus, that together you may with one voice glorify the God and Father of our Lord Jesus Christ. . . . May the God of hope fill you with all joy and peace in believing, so that by the power of the Holy Spirit you may abound in hope. (Italics mine. Rom. 15:5-6, 13.)

There is a sculptured stone on the porch of the cathedral in Chartres which represents God the Father holding Adam in his arms. Adam's head is on his breast, and his feet are drawn up in the shape of a fetus in a mother's womb. He seems to be asleep, with eyes closed in apathy and unconcern, a picture of sloth and dejection. God the Father is looking down at him; and the expression on the sculptured face is one of "infinite tenderness, infinite longing, as though He hoped that Adam might be quickened by His gaze into awakening, opening his eyes recognizing his Father, recognizing how He had held him in His arms, loved him, waited for him, and be swept with a passion to love Him back and to enter into the order of Grace in his relations with his brothers." [11]

For Paul and other vital Christians this is just what they mean by being *in* Christ. Through the influence of the Spirit the fetus comes to life, stretches his limbs, looks up into the Father's face, and freed from guilt and condemnation which have kept him in sleep and self-deception, goes out in the concern of a great love to share this grace with others. In this forgiving love of God is the freedom from apathy and unconcern as well as the other negative sins against our true destiny and the destiny of mankind. To Charles Wesley as well as to Paul it was the sum and solution of the whole mystery of life. From his pen came songs such as "Jesus, Lover of My Soul" and "Love Divine, All Loves Excelling," which pealed out the deliverance of Christ to the burdened and guilt-ridden people in the Great Awakening. Man waking from the sleep of death and looking into the face of Christ sang with exalted joy:

> 'Tis Love! 'tis Love! thou diedst for me!
> I hear thy whisper in my heart;
> The morning breaks, the shadows flee;
> Pure, universal love thou art:
> To me, to all, thy mercies move;
> Thy nature and thy name is Love.

[11] D. V. Steere, *Time to Spare* (New York: Harper & Bros., 1949).

It was the hymn Charles Wesley wanted sung at his own funeral. It was the hymn of those saved from dejection to loving concern:

> Lame as I am, I take the prey;
>   Hell, earth, and sin with ease o'ercome;
> I leap for joy, pursue my way,
>   And, as a bounding hart, fly home;
> Through all eternity to prove
> Thy nature and thy name is Love!

"All right, but let's get down to earth," my disillusioned, cynical, and frustrated reader may rightfully say. "That was in the first century and in the eighteenth century. What about me, now, in the twentieth century?" At the risk of some repetition I want to answer Mr. Cynical-Discouraged by amplifying on two facts which may be experienced in Main Street or Fifth Avenue or Podunk Center any day by anyone who is ready to look at himself as he is and face his guilt in the light of the revelation of God's love in Christ. Chances are our questioner has come the long way of trying by various means to keep from seeing himself, for the "human organism seems capable of enduring anything in the universe except a clear, complete, fully conscious view of one's self as he actually is." [12] (O'Neill's insight in *The Iceman Cometh* is true of us all—before forgiveness we would rather die than to see ourselves as we really are.) But at last, with pride surrendered, flat on his back in the bottom of the abyss, he looks up into the face of Christ; and he begins to understand these two things: First,

We Cannot Forgive Ourselves

No one ever permanently and completely overcomes dejection and frustration with its guilty self-condemnation and self-distrust without first finding the forgiveness of God. This may seem a sweeping statement to make in the face of the dogmatism of those who try to prove that sin and guilt are outmoded mores of a superstitious past. Of course there is no place for forgiveness for those who con-

[12] Sherrill, *op. cit.* Used by permission of John Knox Press.

sider a sense of guilt an excessive morbidity of mind. However, to declare that there is no sin and therefore no guilt does not change the feeling in one's own heart that he has failed. It does not remove the sense of inadequacy. Psychiatrists readily admit that the sense of inadequacy is present, but some limit the cause to lack of social approval and success.[13] This holds for much of our self-distrust but cannot explain the deep consciousness of failure among even the socially successful. It does not account for the fact that we despise ourselves for some of the things we have done and for having failed to live up to even our own ideals, much less those of God. These facts cannot be so easily shrugged off. The simple truth is that we cannot forgive ourselves.

An old Greek drama tells the story of Orestes, who had sinned against his loved ones even to the point of murder, and who was driven about over the face of the earth by the Furies. These vengeance-seeking spirits represent the sense of deep guilt in his own conscience. He tried in every way possible to escape but was unable to find peace until at last he persuaded a jury of his own countrymen to vote him forgiveness. Orestes' experience is typical of every man's experience. He cannot forgive himself.

Sometimes the assurance of others that we no longer need condemn ourselves does help. Psychiatrists are often successful in removing guilt that is morbid and abnormal. But in the darkest hour of man's deepest self-despair only the forgiveness of God can set him free and give him the power to forgive himself.

There is a growing tendency on the part of many who would substitute science for religion to look to the high priest of psychiatry rather than the ministry of the church for relief from the burden of inner failure. T. S. Eliot's play *The Cocktail Party* typifies this approach. Edward, the discouraged husband, is pictured groping in the darkness of the "hell [that] is oneself," unable to love his wife, Lavinia, or to overcome his own self-condemnation. He describes his despair in graphic words:

[13] See Karen Horney, *The Neurotic Personality of Our Time* (New York: W. W. Norton & Co., 1937).

Dejection

There was a door
And I could not open it. I could not touch the handle,
Why could I not walk out of my prison?

.   .   .   .

It was only yesterday
That damnation took place. And now I must live with it
Day by day, hour by hour, forever and ever.[14]

He has not yet found the Savior, but the psychiatrist, Reilly, has salvation for him. Into Edward's hopelessness walks the doctor with an almost omniscient and omnipresent power of untangling the confused web of both Edward and Lavinia's hell; and before the play is over, most of the other participants of the Cocktail Party are made whole.

As the drama comes to its romantic end, Edward and Lavinia are seen bravely facing another cocktail party saying that through Reilly "every moment is a fresh beginning." Their confidence in each other and in themselves is restored, and their minds are at rest.

Surely if there were even one doctor on earth with such divine ability, it would be good news. The drama is a profound satire on the idea of the psychiatrist as all-sufficient high priest and savior. I am grateful, indeed, for all the good that psychiatrists can do for confused and troubled minds; but in my acquaintance with the noble profession I know of no such ready-made, hand-me-down miracles. To repeat the words of C. J. Jung, apart from the person's discovery of a "religious outlook on life—a vital faith, hope and love," no person ever truly walks out of the prison of his inner failure and self-distrust. Psychology can lead us to the gateway of the temple, but only religion can lead us within to an altar where our sins are forgiven and our guilt is purged. As another wise psychiatrist puts it, "There is no science possible to serve as a sign post with the inscription, 'This is the right road.' Science can only give the notice, 'This is not the right way.' And that is a very important

[14] *Op. cit.* Used by permission of Harcourt, Brace & Co., Inc.

129

thing. But religion . . . is man's only possibility to adjust himself to the light." [15]

Only God can forgive sins. True, God's Holy Spirit may work through the doctor and psychiatrist, or the minister, or both (the co-operation of psychiatrists and ministers is to be one of suffering humanity's greatest boons); but it is not chiefly through the cleverness of man that the depths of our inadequacies are plumbed. No one of us can walk out of his prison, saved from the inner damnation of his self-centered hell, except as he is restored by the Spirit of God.

There is a basic reality of our humanity expressed in David's cry of penitence:

> Have mercy on me, O God.
>
> .   .   .   .
>
> For I know my transgressions,
>   and my sin is ever before me.
> Against thee, thee only, have I sinned,
>   and done that which is evil in thy sight.
>   (Ps. 51:1, 3-4.)

And now at last Mr. Cynical-Discouraged comes before this ultimate court of appeals. Realizing his utter inadequacy not only before the court of man's approval but before the everlasting tribunal of divine justice, he cries, "Against thee, thee only, have I sinned." Truly every one of us is "weighed . . . and found wanting" (Dan. 5:27), and nothing can remove our guilt and self-condemnation except the forgiveness of the One whose loving purposes we have shunned and whose merciful goodness we have refused, or as is more often the case, simply neglected. The only real answer to our sense of shame and inadequacy is to stand in the presence of One whose love has borne the weight of our sin and whose forgiveness we are not ashamed to accept. Only then can we believe in ourselves again. Then Mr. Cynical-Discouraged can understand the second part:

[15] Künkel, *op. cit.* Used by permission of Ives, Washburn, Inc.

When God Forgives You, You Can Forgive Yourself

It isn't condemnation we need. No one needs another to point the finger at him and condemn him. If we have failed, if we have sinned, the time comes when we condemn ourselves enough. What we do need is forgiveness and the understanding to accept it without shame.

After we have accepted God's forgiveness, we must forgive ourselves or God's forgiveness is of no effect. Few of us realize that Jesus included the forgiveness of our own selves with the others whom we are to forgive before realizing God's pardon. Of the woman taken in adultery he asked of her accusers, "Woman, where are they?" When told that they were gone, he answered, "Neither do I condemn you; go, and do not sin again" (John 8:10, 11). And the first step in sinning no more is to forgive ourselves.

"Do you mean to say," asked a woman who was having trouble forgetting her past and overcoming her sense of guilt, "that I need to accept the forgiveness of God and then not think about the past any more?" My answer was to quote the words of Paul, "There is therefore now no condemnation for those who are in Christ Jesus," and to interpret for her the glorious truth: If God believes in me, then I ought to believe in myself. If God trusts me enough to forgive me, then I ought to forgive myself—and forget it. This is the long-neglected doctrine of justification by faith—not justified of past wrongs, but justified in the present and able to forget and overcome the past. Not that your past failures will not come to your mind occasionally. Of course they will. But it does mean that they will have no power over you.

Then There Is Hope

"Therefore, since we are justified by faith, we have peace with God through our Lord Jesus Christ. . . . And we rejoice in our hope of sharing the glory of God." (Rom. 5:1-2.) These are the most hopeful words ever spoken. The thing we need in our defeated, frustrated old world is hope. And those who are in Christ Jesus have hope—the *hope of sharing the glory of God.* "[Such] hope maketh not ashamed." (Rom. 5:5 K.J.V.) "More than that, we rejoice in our sufferings, knowing that suffering produces endurance, and endurance produces character, and character produces hope, and hope does not disappoint us, because God's love has been poured into our hearts through the Holy Spirit which has been given to us." (Rom. 5:3-5.)

This hope does not disappoint us. The old saying "while there's life, there's hope" should read "while there's hope, there's life," because where there isn't hope, there can't be much life. Recall those bitter words of Oscar Wilde while incarcerated in Reading Jail in England:

> We did not dare to breathe a prayer,
> Or to give our anguish scope:
> Something was dead in each of us,
> And what was dead was Hope! [16]

The Problem of Insignificance and Meaninglessness

The second great problem which we cannot solve outside of a forgiven relationship with God in Christ is the problem of life's meaninglessness and purposelessness, the feeling that it really doesn't make any difference what one is or does. The shrinking of the size of man and his works in comparison to the vast multiverse about him, the anonymity of modern industrialized existence continually reminding him that he is only a number and not a person, the frustrations of his group goals in the threats of war and other uncertainties, and most of all his own failure to arrive at the superman he had intended—all of these add up to a feeling of utter insignificance and emptiness. What is dead is hope; and when hope is dead or dying, there isn't much chance for constructive life.

It is from "this death" of meaninglessness also that we are delivered by "our hope of sharing the glory of God" (Rom. 5:2).[17] Illustrations of the fresh vigor and productiveness which result from

---

[16] "The Ballad of Reading Gaol."

[17] A more detailed description of the deliverance from the anxiety of meaninglessness will be found in the concluding chapter.

this hope are found on page after page of the New Testament account of the early Christians. Into the universal hopelessness of his people, with their poverty, widespread disease, and slavery to the Roman overlord, Jesus' words and spirit swept like a breath of fresh air in a stale dungeon: "You are the light of the world" (Matt. 5:14). Yes, you poor, persecuted, hungry, insignificant persons, you are the salt of the earth. What an amazing thing to say to such a crowd! And yet the most amazing thing is that over the next few months, as they came to believe in him and then to trust the Father whom he revealed, they came to believe also in his estimate of their value and powers. The result was the greatest miracle of history: A little handful of ordinary people, most of them uneducated, all of them poor and of no consequence in the eyes of the world, turning the world upside down, setting in motion the forces that have produced most of the good in our civilization. A seldom-noticed description of Jesus as the "finger of God" (Luke 11:20) could also be used to describe his followers. One of his last statements according to the Gospel of John was to declare, "As thou didst send me into the world, So I have sent them into the world" (John 17:18). As if to say, "You are the finger of God to do his work, to help fulfill his purposes." This was the hope of glory which they were to share—not a glory of idleness and lazy plenty, for there is no glory in that; but a glory of creative achievement as "fellow workmen for God" (I Cor. 3:9). "You are the body of Christ and individually members of it" (I Cor. 12:27), said Paul in carrying out this same figure. Each of you has a great mission to perform. Even if it is being no more than the little finger of Christ, it is important. "We are ambassadors for Christ." (II Cor. 5:20.) "We are witnesses." (Acts 5:32.) "Thanks be to God, who in Christ always leads us in triumph."

Where else did Paul and the other early Christians get the nerve to believe that anything of positive worth could be done in that evil world in which they lived—the world of Nero and the Caesars, with such indescribable poverty, tyranny, and brutality—especially as they personally were faced with imprisonment or even the arena? They did not fold their hands and wait for God to do it all; neither did they throw up their hands and say, "What the heck!" or, "So what!" There is no frustration in the New Testament.[18] There are tons of courage, but not an ounce of futility. "Thanks be to God, who in Christ always leads us in triumph, and through us spreads the fragrance of the knowledge of him everywhere." (II Cor. 2:14.) This was their secret. The God of steadfast hope and encouragement was filling them with all joy and peace in believing, so that by the power of the Holy Spirit they were abounding in hope. (See Rom. 15:13.)

Then There Is Loving, Vital, Active Concern

The most powerful and impelling motive for good works is not the hope of profit, whether in this life or in heaven; nor is it the fear of hell, defined in what others will think, or the condemnation of one's own conscience, or in a future after death. The most powerful motive for loving deeds is love that constrains and commands a free man's response.

> He who knows Love—becomes Love, and his eyes
>   Behold Love in the heart of everyone,
> Even the loveless: as the light of the sun
> Is one with all it touches. He is wise
> With undivided wisdom, for he lies
>   In Wisdom's arms. His wanderings are done,
> For he has found the Source whence all things run—
> The guerdon of the quest, that satisfies.[19]

Speaking of this divine love as the motive and reason for hopeful action, one of the Friends of God in fifteenth-century Germany in a time of terrific conflict and evil wrote of those who had met and accepted Christ's forgiveness:

There remaineth in them a desire to go forward and get nearer to the

---

[18] They believed in the hope of God relevant to this life on earth as well as at the end of history. The Christian hope contained apocalyptic elements in it, to be sure; but the emphasis remained not in waiting to see what God would do, but in working with him now to make his kingdom realized.

[19] Elsa Barker.

Eternal Goodness ... so that every enlightened man could say: "*I would
fain be to the Eternal Goodness what his own hand is to a man.*" ...
For a true lover of God, loveth Him ... alike in having and in not having, in sweetness and in bitterness, in good and evil report, for he seeketh
alone the honour of God, and not his own, either in spiritual or material
things. *And, therefore, he standeth alike unshaken in all things, at all
seasons.* ... Yea, let them do what they will to such a man, do him wrong
or kindness, bear him love or hatred, yea, if one could kill such a man a
hundred times over, and he always came to life again, he could not but
wish well and do well to him and show him the very greatest kindness in
his power.[20]

The power of the Holy Spirit within us to be the little finger of
God, what a man's hand is to a man; to be faithful to our trust as
we share together in making God's will to "be done, on earth as it
is in heaven"; and even to act in good will toward our enemies—
this is the deep subterranean stream of the water of life that supplies
our need for refreshing courage no matter how dark the night or
how hard the battle. Life never grows stale with a Christlike concern at its center.

From another of the great devotional classics of the same dark
period in Christian history—when the Holy Roman Empire was
breaking up in corruption and warring factions; the leaders of the
church were vain and conscienceless; and those who sincerely
sought to bring some good out of the mess were persecuted and
imprisoned, even burned at the stake—there came these words of
testimony concerning the dynamics of divine love as a motive for
great living:

Love is a great thing, yea, a great and thorough good; by itself, it makes
everything that is heavy, light; and it bears evenly all that is uneven. For
it carries a burden which is no burden, and makes everything that is
bitter, sweet and tasteful. ...
Nothing is sweeter than love, nothing more courageous. ... He that
loveth, flieth, runneth and rejoiceth; he is free and cannot be held in. ...

[20] From *Theologia Germanica*, ed. by T. S. Kepler, 1952, published and copyrighted by The World Publishing Company, Cleveland, Ohio.

Love feels no burden, thinks nothing a trouble, attempts what is above its strength, pleads no excuse of impossibility; for it thinks all things lawful for itself and all things possible. It is therefore able to undertake all things, and it completes many things . . . where he who does not love would faint and lie down.

Love though weary is not tired; though pressed, it is not straitened; though alarmed it is not confounded. . . . But as a lively flame, securely passes through it!

Lest we keep the reference of this victory too much in the Dark Ages of New Testament and medieval times, let us look at an illustration of its triumph in our modern Dark Age. Here is the testimony of an outstanding doctor who later became the famous author of such best sellers as *The Citadel* and *Keys to the Kingdom.* He spent his youth and manhood in England in the period just preceding and following the First and Second World Wars and was infected with the virus of scientism that especially threatened the minds of young doctors, making them believe it was in their power alone to save life and therefore to make life for themselves as they chose. Like many others he maintained the outward form of his Christian faith, but "had little thought of carrying out its tenets and obligations." "If my conscience troubled me, I buried it beneath a mass of worldly interests. While I never openly disowned Christianity—I was too much of a coward to do so—I conveniently forgot about it. I had reached the supreme goal of egoistic existence." That is to say, he was successful, out of the ordinary, in his practice; he was wealthy, respected, healthy, and very wise in his own eyes.

With such a history, at this late stage of self-deception and self-indulgence, it might seem inconceivable that I should have sought peace of mind and soul in returning to my childhood faith. . . . Yet it was not strange to me, for in truth, however much I beat against them, its bars had always enclosed me, and intermittently in my heart, sounding quiet through the tumult of the world, I had heard the echo of that voice which would not be denied. And even when "I fled Him, down the nights and down the days . . . , and under running laughter," I still could hear the beat of those pursuing feet, that secret whisper, "Rise, clasp my hand, and come."

It was not an easy step to take, and one bitter to self-love. For years I had gone on in pride and self-complacency. But that growing interior desolation was irresistible in its compulsion. I stumbled forward, my last defences beaten down, yielded to the craving in my soul. And by whatever means it was accomplished, my period of rebellion against Heaven at last was ended. . . .

Nevertheless, although I did not completely slough my skin, I was conscious, within myself, of a new ease, a sense of relief. There was fresh joy in my work. The sadness, tension, and gnawing ennui which had assailed me all were gone. . . . When I fell down, bludgeoned by my still dominant passions, I picked myself up again, offered my wrists voluntarily, and with true contrition, to the fetters of an active conscience. I had made the immense discovery of why I was alive.[21]

This clear testimony of one man's experience tells how faith, by which one yields at last to the heavenly love, enables the Spirit of God to enter and drive out the seven devils which infest our house of life as a result of our rebellious Sin of self-love and gives us peace and joy, hope and infinite meaning. There is more to be said about how one yields himself to this great forgiveness and keeps growing in relation to the eternal love. It is enough here to declare that dejection, with all its bitter followers, melts like ice in the August sun the day we make the "immense discovery of why [we are] alive!" Then we cry with Washington Gladden, A. J. Cronin, and all others who have accepted their Family relationship:

> O Master, let me walk with Thee
> In lowly paths of service free;
> Tell me Thy secret; help me bear
> The strain of toil, the fret of care.
>
> .   .   .   .
>
> Teach me Thy patience; still with Thee
> In closer, dearer company,

[21] Reprinted by permission of the publisher from A. J. Cronin's *Adventures in Two Worlds*. Published by the McGraw-Hill Book Co., Inc., New York City. Copyright, 1935, 1937, 1938, 1939, 1943, 1946, 1948, 1949, 1950, 1951, 1952, by A. J. Cronin. Reprinted by permission of The Ryerson Press.

In work that keeps faith sweet and strong,
In trust that triumphs over wrong.

In hope that sends a shining ray
Far down the future's broadening way;
In peace that only Thou canst give,
With Thee, O Master, let me live.

Chapter VI

AVARICE

Into Creative Joy—When Things Are Blessed

———◆———

Man is the restless, the hungry, the forever unsatisfied. "We are the hollow men . . . the stuffed men!" We thirst for pleasures and hunger for things to fill our emptiness. We stuff ourselves—our minds, our stomachs, our hours, our barns, our bank accounts. We are sure at first that we can satisfy our cravings by the acquisition of things. We speak of the Almighty Dollar without the slightest suspicion of the irony of such description.

At first the quest for power and place, the joy of possession, is quite exciting. It is like a heady wine as long as the quest is on; and when we reach one goal, we look around for more worlds to conquer. Every new recognition in our field or profession, every new victory over a competitor or in the stock market, makes our blood race. At such times we don't even need to sleep. We are on the way to life's real meaning. This proves our value and importance! This will show them that we are indeed superior ("them" meaning anyone who has doubted our greatness, including our worst doubters—ourselves). The woman shares the excitement with her man. Every time we ride down the street in a new car, we are "bustin' out all over" with satisfaction. And to move into a new house in the most exclusive section of the city is the triumph toward which we strive with panting earnestness.

Like a game that challenges our sporting instincts, the struggle to acquire and possess is an exciting way to feed the fires of self-love.

Of course it is useless to remind one in the white heat of success, or on the way, that there is small profit in gaining the whole world if he loses his own soul. Obviously he is not losing—he is gaining. "This *is* life!" he cries. "What more could you ask?" His armor of self-justification is quite impervious, especially if he has included the church and what he calls "service" in his picture of success. He is living a good life; what more could God want? Don't talk to him about "sin"!

He does not, however, reckon with the fact that the ego god he is serving has the appalling habit of going bankrupt just at the wrong time. Just when you're safest, just when you're "fixed," the whole world suddenly goes to pieces or rises up and threatens to destroy you. Or maybe the betrayal by your self-god doesn't happen overnight, but grows in increasing confusion and conflict. Loved ones or fellow workers get in your way, get sick and die, or betray your trust just when you need them most—or the stock market crashes—or sickness comes to you. The result of your acquisitiveness is not the joy and blessedness you expect, but "headpiece filled with straw." Then you try harder to fill your emptiness.

> Here we go round the prickly pear
> Prickly pear prickly pear,
> Here we go round the prickly pear
> At five o'clock in the morning! [1]

This paraphrase by T. S. Eliot of an old children's game vividly portrays the sin of avarice and its results. Many a person is going round and round the prickly pear at five o'clock in the morning, or at least at seven or eight, and often until ten o'clock at night. Money and bonds, houses and lands, factories and dividends, sought inordinately for security and comfort or for purposes of superiority, are like prickly pears, sharp and uncomfortable when inside of us. Our hunger is insatiable; our thirst is not quenched.

During a recent vacation we took a cruise through some of the

[1] From "The Hollow Men," *Collected Poems*. Used by permission of Harcourt, Brace & Co., Inc.

two hundred miles of canals that make Fort Lauderdale, Florida, the Venice of America. The canals are lined with luxurious homes owned by the wealthy from all over America. Our guide showed a keen sense of humor as he pointed out some especially beautiful homes and told something of the circumstances of their owners. As we glided past one imposing mansion on an island by itself, the guide said, "Mr. ——— of Chicago lives here—that is, for a few weeks each year. He is the president of this company and chairman of the board of that. He has a swimming pool in the center of the beautiful patio. He has a yacht in the back yard, and a Cadillac in the front, and ulcers in his stomach."

There is another interesting scene in Saryoyan's play *The Time of Your Life*, in which Krupp, the discouraged policeman, is talking to Joe in the same waterfront saloon. "I think we're all crazy," he cries. "Here we are in this wonderful world, full of all the wonderful things—here we are—all of us, and look at us. Just look at us. We're crazy. We're nuts. We've got everything, but we always feel lousy and dissatisfied just the same." [2]

Straw in the headpiece! Ulcers in the stomach! Ice in the heart! Misery in the mind! Lousy and dissatisfied! Why this damnation of things? Why is it so many of us cannot enjoy the wealth we have labored so long and hard to acquire? What demon is it that keeps things in the saddle so that they ride mankind instead of being ridden?

There is nothing wrong with things in themselves. Our unconscious inheritance of platonic dualism sometimes tempts us to regard the material world as evil in itself, and we long for the "simple things" of the good old horse and buggy days. We even feel in our gloomiest moments that the ascetic in his cave or Gandhi with his spinning wheel has the answer to our slavery to things. Such asceticism and dualism are a denial of the goodness of the world as God made it. The Hebrew prophet who wrote the first chapter of Genesis declared that God created the world and saw that "it was very good." Money itself is not the root of all evil.

[2] Used by permission of Harcourt, Brace & Co., Inc.

It is the love of money (I Tim. 6:10), the love of the world, with excessive or inordinate desire for acquisition and possession, that to our damnation puts things in the saddle. Avarice is greediness and cupidity, lust after the things of the world, which turns our natural joy in the replenishing of physical needs into a hell of insatiable craving.

Avarice so easily hides from man's careless eyes the real enemy of his joy and contentment. "If only we had another bathroom," . . . "If only we had another car," . . . "If only we had a new refrigerator," . . . "If only we could keep up with the neighbors," . . . "If only we were not pressed for money to buy ample food and clothes," we would be content. So we break the tenth commandment only to be broken ourselves by the results of our covetousness and avarice. Why?

Why is a person avaricious, covetous, and greedy? There are several "too simple" answers which keep too many of us in ignorance of our ignorance. One that has been given by many American political and economic leaders, as well as Marxists of whatever stripe, is the fallacy that greed and avarice will be overcome once a person has sufficient "things" to satisfy him. Man, they say, is an economic being. When he has all the food he can eat, adequate clothing and shelter, he will no longer be greedy and covetous. The trouble is that man can never be satisfied with things. His greed for things is only a reflection of a deeper spiritual lack which he tries to satisfy with the piling up of more and more material securities. "These economic troubles are relatively unimportant. They are not the source of our dilemma. They are merely symptoms. The real trouble lies deeper. We shall never solve our economic troubles till we have solved the dilemma in our spiritual life which produces them." [3]

Read such revealing accounts of life in Russia as Elinor Lipper's *Eleven Years in Soviet Prison Camps* or interview any one of thousands of refugees from the land where all greed and injustice was

[3] John Macmurray, *Freedom in the Modern World* (Chicago: Appleton-Century-Crofts, Inc., 1934).

to be removed by the destruction of private property, and one comes immediately to see the fallacy of this "too simple" answer.

Closely related to this fallacy is the naïve theory of those who believe that man's greed for things is simply a reflection of his will-to-power. Give man a share in social and governmental power, and he will no longer be greedy. Bertrand Russell, who holds to this view, writes, "The desire for commodities, when separated from power and glory, is finite, and can be fully satisfied by a modest competence. . . . When a moderate degree of comfort is assured, both individuals and communities will pursue power and glory rather than wealth. They may seek wealth as a means of power [over men] . . . but the fundamental motive is not economic." [4]

Russell is right in declaring that the underlying motive for greed is not economic, but wrong in saying it is based solely on the desire for power over others. Those persons, even in America, who have succeeded in securing an unusual amount of power over others have not been by any means cured of their greed; but rather the opposite has taken place.

"Love not the world, neither the things that are in the world. If any man love the world, the love of the Father is not in him," writes the author of I John (2:15). One translator makes clearer what this poisonous love means: "Never give your hearts to this world or to any of the things in it. A man cannot love the Father and love the world at the same time." [5] (I John 2:15.)

The sin of avarice is one of the symptoms of man's Sin of misplaced self-love, which rejects or neglects his true relationship with God. Avarice is inordinate self-love seeking to exalt oneself by the possession of things, wealth, and power or to lose oneself and escape from frustration and emptiness through the acquisition of these things.

Avarice is an outgrowth of pride. "And what is pride," asks Augustine, "but a perverse desire of height, in forsaking Him to

---

[4] *Power* (New York: W. W. Norton & Co., 1938).
[5] J. B. Phillips, *Letters to Young Churches* (New York: The Macmillan Co., 1951).

whom the soul ought solely to cleave, as the beginning? This is when it likes itself too well." And Thomas Aquinas declares that the real cause of sin is the "inordinate desire for some temporal good. Now the fact that someone desires a temporal good inordinately is due to the fact that he loves himself inordinately." Because of this "perverse desire of height," brought about by our anxiety over our insecurities, we attempt to make ourselves secure in our own way. We pile up more and more material wealth, forgetting that the day comes when we face the final insecurity of sorrow, tragedy, and death, which we can neither forestall nor prevent and which we had somehow failed to expect. This is the irony of much human life. No matter how much power and temporal goods we possess, we are tempted to pile up more and more of what we call security against the day when no security is enough.[6] "What is fear of need but need itself?" asks the oriental prophet Kahlil Gibran. "Is not dread of thirst . . . the thirst that is unquenchable?"

One can be and often is avaricious while retaining the strictest legal or even moral honesty. Even so, however, it is difficult to claim honesty for those whose barns and bank accounts are bulging while their neighbor suffers great need. The wrong is not so much in the holding of wealth for oneself as in the refusal to use it for the highest good. This is to declare against not the institution of private property, but the failure to use private property as a sacred trust within the family of God to which we belong. The parable of the pounds and the talents, the story of the rich young ruler, and the parable of the rich fool all indicate this central sin. "What shall I do with my goods? I shall tear down my barn and build a bigger barn. No, I shall build not just one barn. I shall build two barns! Three barns! Four barns! Five barns—seven barns! And I will say to my soul, 'Soul, you have ample goods . . . ; take your ease.' "

One of the most revealing parables of the curse of avarice outside of the New Testament is Dostoyevsky's story of the onion as told by the motherly Grushenka in *The Brothers Karamazov:*

[6] See Niebuhr, *op. cit.,* p. 192.

Once upon a time there was a peasant woman and a very wicked woman she was. And she died and did not leave a single good deed behind. The devils caught her and plunged her into the lake of fire. So her guardian angel stood and wondered what good deed of hers he could remember to tell to God: "She once pulled up an onion in her garden," said he, "and gave it to a beggar woman." And God answered: "You take that onion then, hold it out to her in the lake, and let her take hold and be pulled out. And if you can pull her out of the lake, let her come to Paradise, but if the onion breaks, then the woman must stay where she is." The angel ran to the woman and held out the onion to her; "Come," said he, "catch hold and I'll pull you out." And he began cautiously pulling her out. He had just pulled her right out, when the others sinners in the lake, seeing how she was being drawn out, began catching hold of her so as to be pulled out with her. But she was a very wicked woman and she began kicking them. "I'm to be pulled out, not you. It's my onion, not yours." As soon as she said that, the onion broke. And the woman fell into the lake and . . . the angel wept and went away.[7]

This may be only a symbolic story about a future hell, but it is a realistic interpretation of much of the hell of human life. "This is my onion, my goods, my money, my security, by which I—not you—am to be pulled out of my insecurity and exalted and made superior to others." It is this centering upon our own anxiety and seeking to save ourselves at all costs that makes us callous to the deepest needs of God's littlest children all around us, and blinds us to the mighty opportunities to use what we have as good stewards of the mercies of God. The Friends of God in fifteenth-century Germany were right in saying, "Nothing burneth in hell but self-will. Therefore it hath been said, 'Put off thine own will and there will be no hell.' "[8]

The words of the king in Jesus' parable of the final judgment make the basis for rejection of man's prideful claim to righteousness: "I was hungry and you gave me no food, . . . thirsty and you

[7] Part III; Book VII, "Alyosha"; III, "An Onion."
[8] From *Theologia Germanica*, ed. by T. S. Kepler, 1952, published and copyrighted by The World Publishing Company, Cleveland, Ohio.

gave no no drink, . . . naked and you did not clothe me, sick and in prison and you did not visit me. . . . As you did it not to one of the least of these, you did it not to me. . . . Depart from me, you cursed." (Matt. 25:42-43, 45, 41.)

To those who sought to cover up their avarice with occasional deeds of generosity, he cried, "You tithe mint and dill and cummin, and have neglected the weightier matters of the law, justice and mercy and faith. . . . You blind guides, straining out a gnat and swallowing a camel!" (Matt. 23:23-24.)

Swallowing Modern Camels

All the straining at gnats and swallowing of camels was not restricted to the time of Jesus. There are a few embarrassing questions which respectable citizens of civilization today have difficulty in answering, such as: Who is responsible when thousands of troops are slaughtered or critically wounded, not to speak of millions of innocent civilians, all equally precious in the sight of God? Who can say how much of the responsibility for bloody wars is on the shoulders of countless "respectable" people whose avarice shared in or permitted exploitation of other peoples as "lesser breeds without the law"? And what shall we say even of the millions of professing Christians whose avarice or unconcern permits them to give only a pittance to share the gospel of Christian faith and love with other brothers across the seas? Is this the extent of their concern for the neighbor who has fallen among thieves? At the same time they contribute billions of dollars in taxes to pay for the costliness of war. Camels and gnats become confused in their avaricious minds.

Closer home there are countless tragedies of spiritual as well as physical hunger. Lazarus still sits unloved and unhelped at the gate of modern Dives, who "is known far and wide for his generous gifts to the Red Cross and the Community Chest." Doubtless these gifts are of value, but the embarrassing question remains: What kind of world could this be if the eyes of so many "good" people were not blinded by avarice?

What we need is a few realistic pictures revealing our sin in its true colors. We need a modern William Langland, whose *Piers Plowman* described the procession of the seven deadly sins confessing their wrongs, led by "Peronelle, proud heart, cast to the earth," and begging to wear a hair shirt to help her overcome her pride.

> So hungry and hollow-eyed he looked.
> He was beetle browed, and baber lipped
> With his bleared eyes like a blind hag,
> Then came Coveytise [Avarice] whom I cannot describe,
> And as a leathern purse lolled his cheeks
> Wider than his chin, and with age he trembled,
> And as a bondman of his bag on his beard was dedrivelled.
> With a hood on his head, and a dirty hat above,
> And in a tawny tabard coat of twelve winters age,
> All torn and dirty and full of lice creeping.

The modern Avarice would not be dressed in a "tawny tabard coat of twelve winters," but more than likely in a mink coat or a tuxedo, or at least in the longing for one. There are very few misers and hoarders alive today like the man in New York whose house was broken into by the police after he had not been seen for several days. They found him dead in a miser's room filled with every conceivable object, which he had hoarded for twenty-seven years. Most of our hoarding is done in banks and safety deposit vaults, in investments and trusts.

This is not to recommend the opposite sin of prodigality as the salvation from avarice. Dante in the terrace of avarice sees that this sin of wasteful carelessness is also punished. It is not luxurious spending and wastefulness that are needed, but consecrated, intelligent use of things for the best interest of all. Jesus would not have countenanced those who sought to make a virtue of penury and stinginess; he enjoyed good food and was a welcome guest at a wedding party. God the Father made the world and saw that it was good. It is as wrong not to enjoy his provisions and the fine uses to which man's ingenuity has put them as it is to hoard them and seek to make them into a god. Only the concern of divine love within us can keep us open to the best uses of our material world.

Blessed Are They Who Thirst After God

Man is like a mariner becalmed in an ocean of water but starving with thirst.

> Water, water, everywhere,
>   And all the boards did shrink;
> Water, water, everywhere,
>   Nor any drop to drink.

The material things meant for his use and blessing become the accursed means of his devastation when they are made the object of his thirst. Salt water never quenched any man's craving for the fresh, pure water "which comes down from heaven" (John 6:33). So with the craving for the Almighty Dollar. And so with the burning thirst for material security—what an ironical way to speak of the security which is never secure! There is a water which refreshes and enlivens all it touches. Said Jesus to the woman at the well: "Every one who drinks of this water will thirst again, but whoever drinks of the water that I shall give him will never thirst; the water that I shall give him will become in him a spring of water welling up to eternal life" (John 4:13-14). Wise beyond all earthly wisdom is the man who cries, "Give me this water that I may not thirst!"

At the fifth terrace in Purgatory, Dante was deeply moved, almost to despair, as he listened to the confessions of those in whom avarice had wrought such destruction: "Pygmalian, whom his gluttonous thirst of gold made traitor, robber, parricide"; Marcus Crassus, who fell miserably in the Parthian War, though knowing well the "flavour of [his] gold"; Achan in the days of Joshua; Judas, who sold the blood of his Master; and lastly Statius, the friend of Virgil, Dante's guide. Suddenly he felt

148

The mountain tremble; whence an icy chill
Seized on me, as one to death convey'd.

. . . .

Forthwith from every side a shout arose!

The shout was so vehement Dante was overwhelmed, but again and again the sounds swelled: "Glory! . . . Glory in the highest be to God." Dante could not understand.

Never in my breast
Did ignorance so struggle with desire
Of knowledge, . . .
As in that moment. . . .
So on I fared, in thoughtfulness and dread.

As he walked along with his guide, he began to understand the meaning of the shouts and to see that the "natural thirst" of man is never quenched "but from the well whereof the woman of Samaria craved." And the mystery was clearer still to him on the sixth terrace, even before he had seen any evidence of the destruction wrought by gluttony.[9] An angel erased another sin mark "from off my forehead," and the angelic choir sang, "Blessed! [are they which do hunger and thirst after righteousness, for they shall be filled]," and the answering chorus, "I thirst." The whole glorious secret was his as he listened to Statius' response to Virgil's question as to how he was healed:

I enter'd the Parnassian grots, and quaff'd
Of the clear spring: illumined first by thee,
Open'd mine eyes to God. . . . Lo!
A renovated world, Justice return'd,
Times of primeval innocence restored,
And a new race descended from above.

In this dramatic parable of the cleansing of avarice and gluttony Dante follows the experience of Christians in every age. The un-

---

[9] It is interesting to note the close connection here between the sins of avarice and gluttony—two different ways by which man misuses the material world about him.

quenchable thirst after things is never satisfied until it is displaced by a higher thirst. One love displaces another; one thirst makes the other unnecessary. He who seeks continually the glory of God is delivered from the foolish and fatal quest for a false security and exalted self-glory in material things. The Parnassian grots, where the misplaced thirsts of mankind—whether they be for alcoholic stimulants, or the narcotic of ample money in the bank, or the stimulant of buying a whole new wardrobe of clothes—are transformed into a wholesome thirst for the glory of God in man's life and world, are available to every soul who joins with the angelic chorus, saying, "I thirst after God and his rightness."

"What is the chief end of man?" asks the Westminster Catechism. "To glorify God, and to enjoy him forever." This view comes from the recognition that none of these things belong to me; even I myself am not my own; I am his. "I belong to Christ," sang the apostle Paul, "as Christ belongs to God."

All things are yours, whether Paul or Apollos or Cephas or the world or life or death or the present or the future, all are yours; and you are Christ's; and Christ is God's. This is how one should regard us, as servants of Christ and stewards of the mysteries of God. Moreover it is required of stewards that they be found trustworthy. (I Cor. 3:21–4:2.)

This is our Sin: that we have upended the order of our Creator and gone out to glorify ourselves and to enjoy things forever. It will not work! Feeding on the husks that the swine eat never satisfies. Only when we take our rightful and joyous place with the creatures in heaven and earth who do always shout, "Glory! Glory to God in the highest!" do we find possessions and money and material goods belonging to us rather than our belonging to them. You can possess nothing in this world that you hold tightly, rigidly, with the anxious fear that you will lose it. No material thing is blessed in the using that is not held in relaxed, trusting hands. "Consider the lilies, how they grow; they neither toil nor spin. . . . Do not be anxious about your life, what you shall eat, nor about your body, what you shall put on. . . . Instead, seek his kingdom, and these things shall be yours as well." (Luke 12:27, 22, 31.)

All things are yours, even the world and all that is in it, when you look up to God, your Creator, Father, Friend, and Saviour, and ask, "Lord, what is thy will for these things and for me? I rejoice to find that which is true and worthy and fitting; I am hungry and thirsty for thy rightness." Blessed are they who cry, "I thirst after thee, O God!" Augustine's words have a poignancy and meaning here they never had before:

> Thou hast made us for Thyself; and
> Restless are our hearts until they rest in Thee.

The restless soul of man finds his rest in the divine Spirit as a part of the fellowship of the concerned. When he puts the divine family relationships first, he begins to find, as Statius did,

> A renovated world, Justice return'd,
> Times of primeval innocence restored,
> And a new race descended from above.

The fruit of the Spirit is joy—the joy of becoming and being, in which a new perspective of material things provides a true sense of values.

There is a beautiful story of a retired minister who had one favorite song which he delighted to sing at the Wednesday-evening prayer meeting:

> No house, no land do I possess,
> But peace and joy and thankfulness!

At last the laymen of the church got tired of hearing him sing about "no house, no land," so they gave him a house and furnished it. He seemed very happy, but the next week when he arose to sing his favorite song, "No house, no land do I possess," he broke down, unable to go further. The following week the same thing happened. That night, as he stood with his friends who had been so kind to him, he cried, with tears rolling down his cheeks, "Take back the house, take back the furniture, but give me back my song!" This dear man was right. What are houses and lands and bank accounts without your song—the song God intended you to sing, the song of glory which you share with your Father-Creator, not only on sunshiny days, but when the black clouds of seeming tragedy come over you. "The Lord is my strength and my song," sang the Psalmist. "Give me back my song!"

Blessed is he who is hungry and thirsty after righteousness—God's infinitely glorious good—he shall be satisfied. He shall join with the creatures of heaven and earth who do always sing the joyous song: "Glory! Glory to God in the highest!"

Only as new creatures in Christ Jesus will we be able to hold our possessions with a relaxed grip, so that we find joy in using things and know the greater joys of sharing them with others. Only then can we enjoy things and pleasures in their rightful place; or if circumstances require it, dispense with them without grumbling or complaint. Only when we trust and accept the eternal Goodness at the heart of the universe, believing that his riches are inexhaustible and never-failing, will we have no poverty, no unquenchable thirst, no unmet need. Blessed are they who cry, "I thirst after thee, O God!" These are they who can truly say, "The Lord is my shepherd, I shall not want." Here is the faith that saves us from avarice and gluttony, from pride of the eyes and lust of the heart, and lifts us to a calm, joyous existence in which things are used and do not become our masters.[10]

There are many illustrations in every age of this joy in being and using which makes the possessive joys of self-love seem pale in comparison. The clearest revelation of creative joy known to us is the joy of our Lord. Christ stands squarely in the middle of our bored, stale, frantic existence, where jittery nerves and jaded passions take the place of true joy, with an exultant promise which countless thousands of his followers have proved in the most adverse circumstances: "These things I have spoken to you, that my

[10] A fuller treatment of the proper "timing" of life as the result of being in Christ is found in Chapter VII.

joy may be in you, and that your joy may be full" (John 15:11). And yet of all the words of Jesus, modern man is most skeptical of this promise: "my joy." What right did he have to make such a promise? How could one be joyful facing a cross, or poverty and deep sorrow? Multitudes, even among his followers, simply cannot understand these words.

The True Sources of Joy

The first disciples understood what he meant *only* as the perspective of Pentecost enabled them to see the true sources of his joy. They knew that despite his material lack—"Foxes have holes, and birds of the air have nests; but the Son of man has nowhere to lay his head" (Luke 10:58)—his sorrow and suffering, he was the gladdest soul that ever lived. He is the Master of joy, cried the writer to the Hebrews, "who for the joy that was set before him endured the cross, despising the shame" (Heb. 12:2).

His was not an abnormal experience, which only unusually gifted spirits can know, but the normal experience waiting for every soul who overcomes the curse of inordinate love of things and pleasures and learns to glorify God and to enjoy him.

"The fruit of the Spirit is . . . joy," is the description of the experience of the primitive Church. The book of Acts describes the believers as knowing gladness of heart, praising God, and "having favor with all the people" (Acts 2:47). Their neighbors, observing their joy and love, found it so contagious that daily many were added to the Christian community. After the apostles had been beaten and jailed, they went home "rejoicing that they were counted worthy to suffer dishonor for the name" (Acts 6:41). And when the stones pelted young Stephen's brow, it was the joy of his Master which made his face shine "like the face of an angel" (Acts 6:15). "The primitive Church cannot be understood unless full justice is done to this radiance that possessed the believers." [11]

This joy was shared not only by the early disciples but by Chris-

[11] P. G. S. Hopgood, *The Religious Experience of the Primitive Church* (New York: Chas. Scribner's Sons, 1937).

153

tians in every age. Francis of Assisi, living in a day of crass materialism such as ours, was called an apostle of joy. He lived a carefree, yet amazingly helpful life. Having renounced wealth and position, and though afflicted with a disease that kept him in increasing pain, he demonstrated in powerful fashion that joy is an inner treasure which the poorest and the lowliest may possess, and is not dependent upon material possessions, or position, or absence of pain. He and his followers worked with the peasants in the fields, wore the coarsest of garments, slept in haylofts and leper asylums, but went everywhere singing God's praises. Francis said that "sadness belongs not to Christians, but to the devil and his angels."

Such an attitude may be all right for the saints, but what about us common, ordinary people? I would like to testify that the richest heritage of my life is the memory of my mother's joy. The wife of a pioneer New Mexico itinerant preacher whose meager salary was pitifully inadequate even for the primary needs, she patched the clothes of her four children until they could be patched no more. She sent her eldest son to college with nothing but a hope and a prayer and one pair of slick-bottomed dress pants that gave out after the first month. Yet seldom losing her joy that kept her smiling even in her tears, she made us children grow up with the feeling that we were the richest people in the world. Her greatest gift to her children was the conviction that material things in abundance are not necessary for true happiness. None of us grew up with an inordinate craving for security. In her last letter to me before her death at the age of seventy-nine she wrote the secret of her joy: "I still thank God he sent his love into my heart away back there. My heart is flooded with the sunshine of his love. It has carried me over many rough places and will still carry me through this life. Praise his name!"

This is the clearest understanding that I know of the Spirit's deliverance from avarice and the slavery to things. This is what it means to "glorify God, and to enjoy him forever." The source of my mother's joy, and of Francis', as well as the joy of our Lord, was in the living as children of the Father. There is no other way to account for their freedom from the slavery of self and of things except by this confident relationship with the Father.

When we, too, begin to live as sons of the Father, we can enjoy the simple things of life without the sting which so often robs us of these simple satisfactions. Jesus was no grim ascetic, denying the good earth and the good things of human existence. With Browning's David he might have cried,

> How good is man's life, the mere living! how fit to employ
> All the heart and the soul and the senses forever in joy!

One cannot imagine on the lips of Jesus the bitter words of Anatole France: "Life is the result of a disease in the constitution of the planet, a morbid growth, a leprosy, something loathesome, in fact, which would never be found in a well-constituted, healthy star." Rather, Jesus would have joined with George Borrow's gipsy:

"Life is sweet, brother!"
"Do you think so?"
"Think so!—There's night and day, brother, both sweet things; sun, moon and stars, brother, all sweet things; there's likewise a wind on the heath. Life is very sweet, brother."
"In sickness, Jaspar?"
"There's the sun and the stars, brother!"
"In blindness, Jaspar?"
"There's the wind on the heath, brother."

How good is life the mere living, but only when we belong to God and one another! Without this we are unable to enjoy for long even the elemental animal pleasures without bitterness and conflict. Only when the physical and material joys are filled with spiritual meaning do they become precious and worth while.

How May We Enjoy God Forever?

Enjoying God forever is not sentimentality, not merely a poetic phrase; it is a fact of human experience which we too may share. Let us consider three illustrations of its meaning:

1. To enjoy God is to enjoy his creation—all the beauty, majesty, and order of it. God created the earth because of his joy, and when it was done,

> The morning stars sang together,
> and all the sons of God shouted for joy.
>   (Job 38:7.)

You and I are meant not only to contemplate God's creation in wonder and thanksgiving, but to share in it. The fullest joy anyone can know comes when he is creating something with God, as God's partner. The biographies of the most creative lives reveal that they are also the ones who have known the most joy in living.

2. We enjoy God when we find the satisfaction of the needs of the whole self and discover the meaning of life. In seeing and becoming our true selves, we find the deepest joy. We were created to become full-grown persons, after the "measure of the stature of the fullness of Christ" (Eph. 4:13). When we are fulfilling that destiny, we will be joyful. Jesus exulted over the "joy in heaven over one sinner who repents" (Luke 15:7). When a person "comes to himself" and says, "I have been losing myself; this is what I was meant to be," and then begins to become his true self so that he is stronger, better, more creative, than yesterday—that person will share God's joy in that moment. No matter the cost. It will not be too great. The pain and sorrow and grief through which he passes will not be frustrating or bitter. What counts is becoming!

3. Belonging to God as sons in the Father's house, you and I will possess a joy in the service of something which is ultimately and eternally worth while. Cried Rupert Brooke, writing in World War I, "Now, God be thanked, who has matched us with His hour." He found a joy in God in spite of the war—or rather through the war—which was beyond all wars. This is my experience: joy is in meeting a great challenge which commands the best in me. It comes from losing myself in that which I believe eternally worth while. "Personal happiness is functioning for something which you conceive is truly big enough," said Nehru of India. Joy comes not

in the security and safety of money and things, or in satiation with pleasure and comfort. It comes in meeting the storms and battles fully confident of ultimate victory, in confronting the biggest dare one can find and becoming a cocreator with God.

Von Hügel, great Christian saint, in the last few minutes of his life said to his niece, "Christianity taught us to care. Caring is the greatest thing. Caring matters most." "Through suffering he discovered joy, and to his final note of joy he added love." He knew it is the care of this loving Father which holds us steady, which lifts us out of the miserable self-pity and inordinate self-love which keeps things in the saddle and makes it possible for us to care. For joy and love go hand in hand together. This is the everlasting food and drink, unpriced, which will be denied no person who is willing to accept it.

Blessed are they who hunger and thirst after God and his rightness; they shall be satisfied. From their deep joy shall come an "endless, endless hallelujah."

Chapter VII

LUST and GLUTTONY

Into Timed Living—When Pleasure Is Good

———————◆———————

Vanity, vanity, all is vanity
That's any fun at all for humanity . . .
Oh worra, worra! Rooted in Sodom and Gomorrah! [1]

Why is it that the things you enjoy most are always sin?"
asks a character in a favorite American play.

And from a popular record a crooner groans that anything that
is so much fun must be illicit, must be against the law. It seems
to him that this is an "age that curbs all pleasure," so anything that
makes you feel so good must surely have in it somewhere a "hidden
flaw."

The confusion back of these quotations from current Ameri-
cana underlines the reason for much of the futility in human
life. For the man or woman on the street, or in the shop or office, or
down on the farm, there is not much enthusiasm for the Stoic
motto "Know thyself." Self-knowledge is too much bother, too
costly. Most of us do not really want to know ourselves. For the
Epicurean motto "Enjoy thyself," however, the average man or
woman can work up a great deal of enthusiasm. The trouble, it
seems to him, is that religion and conscience, the law and customs,
are all conspiring against his self-enjoyment, which he generally as-
sociates with the body and its sensations.

[1] Ogden Nash, *Many Long Years Ago*. Used by permission of Little, Brown & Co.

Surveying our earthly advertisements, novels, plays, movies, and conversation, a Martian visitor could easily describe the Body Beautiful as the goddess whom most Westerners worship as passionately as the Greeks did Venus. More money is spent each year on beautifying the body and keeping it healthy and attractive than on all mental and spiritual education and religion. Why not? Man is chiefly animal, according to the generally accepted theory. While the masses wouldn't argue the point about man's animal nature, most of them give mental assent to the theory that man does have a soul which will be put into use at death, they hope. Nevertheless they proceed upon the assumption that man's best moments come when he lets himself go, doing what comes naturally. This quest for sensual enjoyment has become the chief religion of modern man —though the glorification of things would run it a close second— if by religion one means that set of values to which one gives fullest allegiance. Great multitudes worship daily at the altars of this sensualist religion, in theaters, on the beaches, and in their homes. Early and medieval Christians called this the sin of luxury, from which we get our word "lust." It meant being excessively desirous of sensual experiences that gratify the appetite or tastes—to luxuriate in earthly food, dress, and sex. Of course today such an attitude would be considered a relic of the past and outmoded. Aesthetics is a more pleasing name for this sensualist religion: art for art's sake, beauty for beauty's sake, the body for the body's sake. This is all the meaning there is in life and all there needs to be.

And certainly as contrasted with a religion that seeks to reduce our enjoyment and use of the physical to the bare minimum and eliminate it as soon as possible, aestheticism does seem to open the doorway to life. It is sad indeed that the Christian religion has been associated with the former kind of religion and regarded as a joy-killer, so that the things one enjoys most are always considered sinful.

The religion of the Body Beautiful and Enjoyed often has a greater appeal to youth or to those who would stay young than the religion of Glorifying Things (which moralists call avarice). Both stem from the same root. A fifteenth-century English morality play, *The Castle of Perseverance*, describes the conflict between the virtues and the sins of mankind. It closes with Mankind having been shut out of the castle by Lust, Sloth, and his other sins until as an old man when "time cools the heat of youth and passion" he is enticed by Covetousness. "Covetousness, whither should I wend?" he asks. "What can I expect from you?"

> I begin to wax hoary and cold;
> My back beginneth to bow and bend,
> I crawl and creep and wax all cold!

This is the principal drawback to the religion of aesthetics. Its devotion pays lesser and lesser dividends until the time comes when its devotee finds himself

> . . . in an unquiet world
> For [him] the way has become too long, the road
> Precarious and painful, the colours greyed,
> The sounds too faint and far for his faded sense.
> And there is only the dread of living longer,
> And the terrible ancient eagerness for earth
> To stop his ears and seal his eyelids shut
> Within a womb from which no way returned.[2]

When one has accepted the ultimate hopelessness of life without God, as the Bible realistically calls it, the logic of sensualism is strong enough. The most popular quotations of philosophers who have no living faith in God are the words of the ancient Chinese, "Enjoy yourself; it's later than you think," and the Epicurean, "Eat, drink, and be merry; for tomorrow you die." If life's deepest joy and greatest happiness exist in draining every bit of sensation

[2] From *The Seven Sins* by Audrey Wurdemann—used by permission of Harper & Brothers.

possible before the time comes when you are unable to enjoy anything, then why not major in pleasure? Why should such enjoyment be called sin?

The answer of the secularist is to wave the hand and say with vigorous indignation, "Bosh! To enjoy yourself is not sin. You are suffering from the superstitions of an unenlightened past. It is only the nonsense of outmoded religion that speaks of sin. Forget it! Enjoy yourself while you can."

Nietzsche, as the most outspoken of modern Dionysians,[3] poked fun at those who spoke satirically of him as one who "walketh amongst us as if amongst animals." His answer was to go them one better:

It is better said in this wise: "The discerning one walketh amongst men AS amongst animals."

Man himself is to the discerning one: the animal with the red cheeks.

How hath it happened unto him? (this unhappy state of concern about excess in drink, sex, etc.) Is it not because he hath had to be ashamed too oft?

Oh, my friends! Thus speaketh the discerning one: shame, shame, shame—this is the history of man! . . .

Verily I like them not, the merciful ones, whose bliss is in their pity. . . .

Verily I have done this and that for the afflicted; but something better did I always seem to do when I had learned to enjoy myself better. Since humanity came into being, man hath enjoyed himself too little: that alone, my brethren, is our original sin.[4]

This is the trouble with man, echo many psychiatrists and sociologists. He has been repressing his desires from the time of babyhood and feeling ashamed because of his natural functions and passions. What he needs to do is to express himself completely, without restraint except for certain social graces which must be

---

[3] Dionysus was a Greek god around whom was built a vitalistic cult celebrating the joys of physical sensations as the end of life.

[4] From *Thus Spake Zarathustra*. Everyman's Library. Published by E. P. Dutton & Co., Inc. Used by permission of J. M. Dent & Sons, Ltd.

condoned temporarily until all shame has been driven from his mind.

One fly in the ointment, however, according to the history of the human race in general as well as the experience of everyone of us in particular, is the fact that the more wholeheartedly you throw yourself into the quest for enjoyment, the less joy you get out of it. Whether taste or feeling, the more you feel the less you feel. To be surfeited or satiated with feeling is the reward of the one who makes sensuous feeling his prime objective. In the long run—and it may not take longer than middle age or even late youth—he will understand the bitter cry of Lord Byron, who in the prime of his life with all the opportunities for aesthetic enjoyment possible for any human being cried:

> My days are in the yellow leaf;
>   The flowers and fruits of love are gone;
> The worm, the canker, and the grief
>   Are mine alone!

There is keen insight in the story of the young man who came to a renowned doctor in Paris complaining of dejection and nausea at life, and asking what he could do to get well. The doctor with a trace of envy pictured the happy state of the young blade Grimaldi, who was leader of the younger set in Paris night clubs. "Go to him," said the doctor; "let him show you how to enjoy yourself, and you will get well." The downcast young patient looked up with a sardonic smile and said, "I am Grimaldi."

There are other flies, too, in the ointment of pleasure for pleasure's sake. Not only does lust lose its luster and taste its tang as we seek primarily to enjoy ourselves, but there is the even more disastrous fact that sooner or later with no greater goal in life we become slaves to our lusts and appetites. We destroy our minds and bodies and the precious relationships of love. As Dante is purported to have said concerning the sin of lust,

> The bond of friendship breaks and brotherhood,
> At variance still with Truth and Reason's light.

Like all other symptoms of man's Sin lust is irrational. "It is crazy for me to do this," said one young man, "but I've got to, anyway!" This is the experience that in popular parlance is supposed to be bigger than you are. And it *is* bigger than they who are afraid or unwilling to accept their places as sons of God.

No, it isn't the Christian religion that is to blame for our shameful use of the body—not the mere calling of an act a "sin." It is within me, that something (my Sin of misplaced self-love) which puts a shadow on the brightness of day and a pallor on the rosiest cheek, and lays a curse on the body which I seek to exalt and beautify and makes it ugly and repulsive. *This death!* How far its tentacles reach! It extends even into the innocence of man's natural enjoyments and corrupts them so that what should be the sweet accompaniment of love and life becomes the harrowing discord of hate and death.

There are three ways in which man's Sin of prideful self-love takes the good which rightfully belongs to the body and makes it evil: first, the attempt of self-righteous religion to eliminate the physical and to abolish pleasure; second, the attempt of self-loving aestheticism to exalt the self through gratification of the senses; and third, the attempt to escape the prison house of self, with its confusions and futility, into nothingness.

The Evils of Self-Righteous Puritanism

It must be admitted that the emphasis placed by many Christians in every age upon what has come to be known as "puritanism" [5] is responsible for the idea that all physical pleasure and enjoyment are sinful because they are pleasurable. This idea was a carry-over from Hellenistic thought and did not belong to the true Hebrew-Christian tradition. The assumption concerning the place and value of the body which is distinctly Christian is best described in the words of Genesis 1:

[5] An unfortunate use of the word, for much that is good and worthy in our American life came from the Puritans.

So God created man in his own image; . . . male and female he created them. And God blessed them, and God said to them, "Be fruitful and multiply, and fill the earth and subdue it; and have dominion." . . . And God saw everything that he had made, and behold, it was very good. (Gen. 1:27-28, 31.)

Jesus accepted this conception of the basic unity between soul and body not only in his teachings but in his actions. He reaffirmed the Deuteronomic summary of the law: you are to love God not only with all your soul and mind but also with all your bodily strength and vigor. Jesus was at home in the festivities of a wedding and enjoyed eating with his friends. The Pharisees, who had begun to identify religious superiority with ascetic fasting, accused him of being a "glutton and a drunkard" (Matt. 11:19) because he refused to wear a long face. The falsity of their charge needs no proof. As pointed out in the preceding chapter, as clear as any one fact we know about him is the fact that he enjoyed life. When he said, "I came that they may have life, and have it abundantly" (John 10:10), he surely did not mean that life is found in the enjoyment of physical pleasures; neither did he mean that life is found in the denial of physical pleasures. It is a blasphemy on his character and life to insist that for his followers everything that is pleasurable is sin because it is pleasurable.

Nevertheless this is exactly what happened when Christian theologians such as Origen and Clement of Alexandria tried to harmonize the Greek philosophy of dualism between body and spirit with Christianity. Origen interpreted the story of the fall as a literal seduction by the serpent of Eve, and therefore original sin was an inclination "to ignominy and wantonness." Clement of Alexandria described the fall as a "falling under the power of pleasure, for by the serpent pleasure creeping on its belly is in a figure signified."

It is impossible to estimate how much harm this has done in preventing millions of people from understanding and accepting the abundant life offered in the Christian gospel. The idea that sensual pleasure is itself sinful became a perfect vehicle for the expression

164

of self-righteousness. It also lead to hurtful repression which has rightfully become the object of disgust and approbrium among those trained in the more realistic understandings of modern psychology. It gave Nietzsche his ground for saying that

> chastity is a virtue with some but with many almost a vice. These are continent to be sure; but doggish lust looketh enviously out of all that they do. Even into the heights of their virtue and into their cold spirit doth this creature follow them, with its discord. And how nicely can doggish lust beg for a piece of spirit when a piece of flesh is denied! [6]

Nietzsche along with modern psychiatrists was right in declaring the evils committed by those who repress their sensual desires. There have been in every age of Christian history the hard, cold bitterness and cruelty of self-righteous "puritans" attempting to prove their superiority to others by their abstinence from overt acts of sensuality, while at the same time they were seeking to injure those who "sinfully" continued to enjoy any pleasure. The witch burnings in the seventeenth century were of the same spirit as the unchristian gossip and social ostracism committed in our own times by those who consider their ill temper and pride minor sins as compared to the sins of drunkenness and adultery, which they condemn. To these evils could be added the thousand and one private ills of body and mind that are caused by repression. There is also the disruption of the proper expression of human love which produces marital discords. "How nicely can doggish lust beg for a piece of spirit when a piece of flesh is denied!" Still relevant to our own time was Jesus' insight when he said to the Pharisees who had flung at his feet the woman taken in adultery: "Let him who is without sin among you be the first to throw a stone at her" (John 8:7). Surely the cold mercilessness and hardheartedness of the outwardly chaste Pharisee is as sinful as the lustful search for self-exaltation and self-forgetfulness of the socially disapproved sensualist.

A word needs to be said here concerning the difference between

---

[6] From *Thus Spake Zarathustra*. Everyman's Library. Published by E. P. Dutton & Co., Inc. Used by permission of J. M. Dent & Sons, Ltd.

repression and suppression, which have been borrowed from the technical language of the psychiatrist. The true Christian does not repress his physical desires and passions. Neither does he express them just any time he feels them. To do the former would be dishonest and destructive; to do the latter would be to make himself a slave of his passions and thus to suffer from "this death" of lust. One who has accepted the blessed relationship as a member of the family of God will use his body "not in rioting and drunkenness, not in chambering and wantonness, not in strife and envying"; but putting on the Lord Jesus Christ, he will "make not provision for the flesh, to fulfill the lusts thereof" (Rom. 13:13-14). That is, he will give no opportunity for the lusts of the flesh to enslave him because he has put on the spirit of the Lord Jesus.[7] What then does a Christian, who puts on the spirit of Christ, do if he doesn't repress his desires when the situation is not appropriate for Christlike expression of these desires? The answer is that he suppresses his desires for the time being. Repression is unconscious refusal to recognize the desires, and rejection of them. Suppression is conscious admission that one feels the desire and the conscious decision that the highest good is served by refusing to entertain the desire longer or to carry the desire to its logical conclusion in the overt act. It is repression which produces the neuroses and mental illness from which proceed irritation, mercilessness, hard cruelty, and even physical ills. Suppression of natural desires, when done in the right spirit, can be the means of sublimating the desires and using the physical instincts as a strong basis for other creative activities. Christian chastity, therefore, is not innocence; but, as Thomas Mann describes Joseph in Egypt,

His famous chastity was so far from being due to inexperience that it was closer to the opposite: resting rather upon a feeling that the mutual relations between him and all the world were permeated with the spirit of love; he was in love with everything, with a love deserving of the adjective universal, because it did not stop at the earthly but was

[7] What this means will be more fully described in the last part of this chapter.

present as a pervasive atmosphere, as an inference, a subtle significance and unconscious background to every relation in life, even the holiest and most awe-inspiring. From this feeling his chastity proceeded.[8]

Joseph suppressed his natural human passions in rejecting the temptation of Potiphar's wife because of his *agape* love which included her best interests as well as his own and those of his master, Potiphar. He could not express his desires and thus sin against the divine love of God which put him in a family relationship with these his fellow beings. Such suppression of physical desire did not injure him, but rather became the creative background out of which he lived a noble and divinely useful life.

When Is Pleasure Evil?

Pleasure is evil only when it is used to assert and exalt the ego-image of my self-love or when it is used to cover up and escape from the confusions and frustrations of my anxious failures to realize the goal of my self-dream or to allay the fears of death and the beyond. Pleasure is neither good nor evil within itself. It becomes either evil or good depending on the spiritual use to which it is put. There is the pleasure felt in the satisfaction of painful tension, such as the relief of hunger, thirst, or sexual desire. There is also the pleasure that comes from revenge. Others have hurt you, or you have hurt yourself, and you get revenge. "Sadism" is the word for the pleasure in hurting others, "masochism" for hurting yourself. Obviously the pleasure in hurting others or from our own hurt is an abnormal kind of pleasure which signifies the desperate attempt to preserve and keep our ego-image or, failing to do so, to overcome our sense of guilt and failure. Hickey, the drunken salesman in O'Neill's play *The Iceman Cometh*, is a perfect illustration of both kinds of abnormal pleasure. It had been his custom to show up at periodic intervals at a certain low-grade saloon where he spent a night in drunken forgetfulness with a motley crowd of other drunks. On this occasion he was seemingly sober and at peace for

[8] *Joseph in Egypt* (New York: Alfred A. Knopf, 1938). Used by permission of the publisher.

the first time. Though he was willing to buy drinks for the old gang, he much preferred to save them from their pipe dreams, as he himself claimed to have been saved. It was soon evident, however, that this Hickey brand of salvation was not salvation at all but the renunciation of all hopes (pipe dreams). One arrived at it by realizing and admitting exactly how one felt instead of kidding oneself. The Hickey salvation of O'Neill's play is a parody on the salvation offered by popular psychology which declares: Admit your desires and express them and you will be happy. Get rid of your pipe dreams. Do what you want to do, and you will have real peace.

But the peace he was talking about turned out to be the peace of death. For years he had hurt his wife by continually coming in drunk and being unfaithful to her. Evidently hers was an *agape* love which always forgave him and expressed her confidence that his protestations of good intention would be lived up to "this time." Being unwilling to surrender the ego-image of himself which alcohol helped him temporarily to exalt, he was unable to be true to her or to cease his drunken sprees. Her forgiveness made him feel more guilty and hate himself more and more. This continued until the twisted reasoning of his guilty and frustrated mind led him to kill her. He said he did it because he loved her, but in an off-guard moment he described how he laughed over her dead body and said what he had long wanted to say: "Well, you know what you can do with your pipe dream now!" [9] His strange peace was the result of his abnormal pleasure in getting even with one he had hated for so long even though he claimed to love her. He did not love her of course. The true self within him longed to respond to her love, but what he really loved was his own pipe dream which alcohol and "tarts" helped him to satisfy for a while. She had not stood in his way except by making him feel guilty. Hence the pleasure at her death and the relief at being able to drink himself into complete nothingness without even her love to prevent. The play ends with all the drunken bums relieved of the false salvation Hickey had tried to force on them, rejoicing in the last words

[9] Used by permission of Random House.

their friend said as the detectives led him away to stand trial for the murder of his wife: "I haven't got a single . . . lying hope or pipe dream left!" [10] The curtain falls with all of them drinking desperately with the determination to "knock ourselves out," to get "cockeyed" and "paralyzed."

Here is a parable of the kind of spirit that makes pleasure a deadly evil. Hickey and all other alcoholics, adulterers, and gluttons begin their misuse of bodily sensations for the purpose of exalting themselves through pleasure in the gratification of their senses, but end up by using the same methods in an effort to escape from the self they now hate.

The sin of sensuality is the inordinate love of pleasure as a means either of exalting and asserting one's self-love or of escaping and destroying the self that has betrayed one. Sensualism is physical, sensual enjoyment without *agape* love; therefore it enslaves and inhibits rather than sets free as it claims to do.

One way to discover whether or not a pleasure, which could be good in the right place, is evil as one is using it is to ask, "Is this something I feel I *must* have, that I can't do without, even if some higher good demands that I do so?" No doubt it will require a great deal of honesty to be able to answer this question. But it points to the difference between a "scarcity pleasure" and an "abundance pleasure." The scarcity pleasure is one in which some physical or psychical lack is satisfied, while the abundance pleasure is one in which the satisfaction is not a necessity, but an expression of our human freedom and creativeness. When one is lacking in inner security and attempts to cover it up by possessive love, the result is always hate and more and more insecurity. Then, though our actual physical wants are satisfied, we are still filled with craving. Pleasure, when it becomes scarcity pleasure, never satisfies. Eating too much, drinking alcoholic stimulants, the use of narcotics, and promiscuous sex activity are all means by which one seeks to hide his insecurity and elevate his ego feelings. The result is increased guilt and insecurity and hatred toward those who get in the way,

[10] *Ibid.*

even toward those who love and forgive us. This in turn results in masochism and sadism by which we seek the pleasure of hurting and destroying ourselves and them. This kind of quest for pleasure is evil and self-destructive, and is an indication of failure to understand the basic facts of human existence and to relate life in trusting love to the love of God.

Why We Overeat

This explanation should help us understand why some of us continue to eat too much even though the doctor tells us it is hurting our health and may lead to our death. We begin overeating as a means of satisfying some deep inner craving. Food does not fill our emptiness, but tasting and eating seem to be necessary. Put it this way: we can stand our emptiness, or spiritual confusion, when we are eating better than when our stomachs are empty. It is a well-known fact among doctors that their patients suffering from obesity with but few exceptions are those who eat because of some neurotic need which has not been satisfied. And they will agree with you privately that those who continue in spite of repeated warnings to "dig their graves with their teeth" are literally so dissatisfied with themselves and with life that they really don't care. The vital concern of *agape* love is missing within them or, if present at all, is only an occasional glimmer. They need the satisfaction of increasing amounts of rich food or of stimulating drink to keep going.

All of us know this principle from experience, though on a much-less-intense scale. When we are disgusted or irritated about something, we are far more likely to eat too much or give way to our pet indulgence whatever it may be, whether sex, liquor, or excessive smoking. It is when one lets down from some central and worthy purpose that he turns to animal satisfactions and artificial stimulants. The point which many doctors miss is that we do not really

---

[11] The use of alcoholic stimulants is in a separate category from the sin of overeating in that any pleasure thus derived is both unnatural and illusory and leads to damage not only to myself but to others.

cure ourselves of our overeating or alcoholism [11] or promiscuity—not by diets or by changing scenery or by any other means. We learn to use the good pleasures of life in their time and place and to refuse the hurtful pleasures that poison and anesthetize us *when* we have begun to be delivered from our central Sin of misplaced self-love and to enter the saving relationship of loving security with the Spirit of God. When I am free of the demand to exalt myself or to provide some artificial security against my desperate insecurity, then I can use the simple pleasures of life to add color and romance to the abundance of life which is mine. "To him that hath [security] shall be given [real joy and satisfaction]; but to him that hath not [security and meaningful purpose and love] from him shall be taken away even what he hath [even his ability to enjoy the simple pleasures of life]." This paraphrase of Jesus' words declares what he was ever making the central theme of his teaching: when man loses himself in a living faith in the love of God, he finds himself. But having lost the true center of his life—the love of God—he cannot be master even of his own will as the center of himself. This is the reason our wills seem to be powerless to keep us from drinking or eating to our own hurt as well as to the hurt of our loved ones.

The Misuse of Sex

An understanding of the Sin of misplaced self-love also explains the misuse of sex and points to the way in which it may be kept sacred and beautiful. There is one difference, however, between these sins of sensualism. Eating and drinking are a more personal, individual matter than is sex, though indirectly of course they all affect others as well as ourselves. Sex represents the need for a high degree of community between two persons, such as no other human experience requires. Perhaps this is the reason many Christians have considered sexual sins as the worst kind of sins, for our sexual needs provide the best opportunity for self-assertion as well as self-pleasing. Sex becomes evil when it is the means by which one person preys on another, "as it is . . . among the spiders where the bride

171

concludes her nuptials by eating her groom." [12] These attempts at self-assertion may lessen or completely destroy the blissful sense of belonging to each other which sexual union gives at its best. When the sex act is principally the expression of self-love, it is self-defeating. When one seeks through it the domination of the other or the pure gratification of one's own desires, the deepest pleasure is impossible. Instead the opposite of pleasure—the deepest suffering—is likely. When, on the other hand, the expression of sexual desire is accompanied by *agape* love, tenderly concerned for the well-being and enjoyment of the other, only then does it become the creative union of two spirits as well as two bodies. In fact, without this *agape* love even the fullest union of the two bodies is impossible. Suspicion, mistrust, resentment, hostility, jealousy, envy—any of these sins of self-love serve effectively to destroy harmony of bodily functions and result in unnatural frigidity and accompanying frustration. Physical harmony at its best is impossible apart from spiritual harmony. This fact underlies the truth that the sex act even in marriage may be sinful and destructive rather than creative and rewarding.

Whatever viewpoint is taken concerning the merit of the Kinsey Report on the *Sexual Behavior in the Human Female*, the report unquestionably emphasizes this very fact—that harmonious relations between men and women are dependent on mental and psychological factors more than on the physical alone. It claims to prove, as one reviewer puts it, what every marriage counselor has suspected, that sexual relations "have been anything but a howling success in the past, all the romantic and oversensual atmosphere of our times to the contrary notwithstanding. They cannot be an easy success because of the very nature of the physical and psychological differences involved. And only greater knowledge, understanding and sympathy on both sides seem to hold much hope for betterment." [13]

This is to say, in terms used in these pages, that real sexual satisfactions are impossible on any other basis than that of *agape* love.

[12] C. S. Lewis, *Screwtape Letters* (New York: The Macmillan Co., 1943).
[13] Ernest Haveman, "The Kinsey Report," *Life*, Aug. 24, 1953.

The Great Superstition of the twentieth century is thus exploded. This superstition has declared, and millions have believed it, that somewhere there is a perfect mate with whom one may be deliriously happy in the perpetual enjoyment of sex satisfactions. The Kinsey Report has done at least this much good along with the tremendous amount of harm in its advocacy (intended or unintended) of "liberty in love." It has shown that "all are more or less in the same boat on these troubled waters," and that there is no such perfect physical mate, but that real physical harmony depends on "understanding and sympathy."

This also is the reason that sexual intercourse outside of marriage is basically wrong, Kinsey, Havelock Ellis, and other advocates of so-called "free love" to the contrary—not because of social taboos, as the "new psychology" insists. The social conventions in a monogamic society have been established as the result of centuries of human experience of the devastation wrought by promiscuous sex activity. Free love, as it is called, is never *agape* love expressing our concern for the well-being of the other as well as for our own highest good; for free love seeks the enjoyment and pleasure of sexual relationships without the responsibilities thereof. It prevents the sympathy and understanding necessary for sexual union. It is the means by which two people use each other's bodies to satisfy their passions without incurring the costly necessity to care for and to be responsible for each other. Free love is free from responsibility and therefore free from the true joy of belonging to each other, which is the spiritual center of real sex satisfaction. Such free love is a prostitution of the true purposes of our sexual capacities. These purposes are not only for the reproduction of ourselves biologically, but for the creation of new relationships of harmony and outgoing affection between two people who have upon their shoulders the building of a home and family life through which little children may first sense the belongingness of the divine family relations. Here in the relation of man and wife is the basis for security or insecurity, for possessive, erotic love only or for affirmative, *agape*

173

love that grows more beautiful and rewarding as the years pass and which redeems and makes sacred even erotic love.

Sexual love that is only *eros* is sin wherever it is. Sexual love that is an expression not only of *eros* but of divine *agape* within our human relationships is always right and beautiful. Free love is sinful because one is not really concerned with what happens to the other. The inevitable sense of guilt, even among those who consider themselves freed of superstitious moral taboos, is one of the best evidences of the unsatisfying and hurtful results of *eros* love. The uneasy conscience, in spite of attempts to hush its voice, says that something is wrong with the relationship.

One of the characteristics of sexual love when it is purely *eros* is the deification of the love partner, by which we seek to escape this uneasiness of self-deification. The expressions of romantic love which are found in many of our popular songs, such as "My Angel," "Girl of My Dreams," and "Dream Lover," are descriptive of the kind of romantic love

in which attributes of perfection are assigned to the partner of love, beyond the capacities of any human being to bear, and therefore the cause of inevitable disillusionment. While the more active part of the male and the more passive part of the female in the relation of the sexes may seem to point to self-deification as the particular sin of the male and the idolatry of the other as the particular temptation of the woman in the sexual act, yet both elements of sin are undoubtedly involved in both sexes.[14]

"My Angel" is seen without make-up to be filled with ugly imperfections of mind and heart as well as body, and the "Girl of My Dreams" turns out to be too often a nightmare of childish anger and selfishness. She has the same experience with her "Dream Lover" or "White Knight," and soon they decide the marriage is impossible. They are "incompatible," to use the convenient phrase of the divorce court. They get a divorce and then search for another woman or man to "idolize." It is only when both partners realize

[14] Niebuhr, *op. cit.* Used by permission of Charles Scribner's Sons.

their own imperfections and give supreme allegiance to the true love of God that they are able to love each other with understanding and sympathy in spite of their imperfections.

When we are disillusioned with ourselves and with the one we set up as a god, we attempt to use sexual passion just as others use drunkenness, as an anodyne, by which we seek to escape and forget the futilities of life. Commercialized prostitution is used without any personal considerations whatever, as a "flight . . . not to a false god but to nothingness." [15]

In summary, sexual desire becomes lust, one of the symptoms of misplaced self-love, when one admits and expresses it either (1) with the intention of asserting oneself in the domination of another to prove one's superiority and to get release from the anxiety of insecurity and inferiority, (2) with the intention of escaping from oneself by making the sex partner an idol, or (3) with the intention of forgetting and escaping into nothingness. On the other hand, sexual desire is beautiful and sacred either (1) when it is freely admitted and suppressed in the conscious mind because to express it would result in harm to oneself or to others in the human relationship, and it is sublimated instead by *agape* love in other creative and productive acts; or (2) when it is freely admitted and expressed in the conscious relationship of *agape* love between two persons who have been joined by God in the creative responsibility of being helpmates for each other in producing a home where divine security and companionship are most easily known.

Riding the Goat

The enjoyment of physical beauty and pleasure is always good when it is not to excess and not a substitute for genuine loving. It becomes evil only when out of its context and when it prevents a higher relationship of *agape* love. It is the lust of self-love that prevents us from enjoying ourselves in that which is rightfully ours and robs us of the highest joys, while it also places a curse of trouble and suffering on others. No wonder in medieval literature lechery

[15] *Ibid.*

was usually symbolized by a goat, from which is derived our expression of disgust and futility "riding the goat." Spenser's *Faerie Queene* pictures Lechery's steed as this silly animal. In Lechery's hand is a burning heart; and dressed in green, he looks very much like the goat which bears him. The burning heart signifies the lust that is never satisfied. Gluttony, with large belly, swollen eyes, bestial look, is mounted on a filthy swine. He is clad like Bacchus in vine leaves and ivy, suffers from dropsy, and carries a "bouzing can" in one hand. Dunbar describes Lechery as "that loathly corse," which "came neighing like a bagit horse."

> Then the foul monster Gluttony,
> Of womb insatiable and greedy,
> To dance he did him dress.
> Him followed many foul drunkard....
> In surfeit and excess.
> Full many a waist-less wallydrag,
> With wames unwieldy, did forth wag,
> In grease that did increase.
> Drink! aye they cried with many a gape
> The fiends gave them hot lead to lap;
> Their thirst was none the less.

How does one quit riding the goat so that one's thirst is quenched and one's passion is directed into creative, loving channels? How often has this question been asked in despair! How can I be temperate in the indulgence of my physical appetites and self-controlled in the direction of my passions? The history of the race and of each of us personally declares the same thing: not merely by the conscious determination to practice the virtue of temperance and self-control, but by yielding to a new relationship of love for God and all men within the divine family.

The root meaning of intemperance is life with its powers out of control. According to Webster's dictionary intemperance means literally the "inability to fit together in due proportions." It is not only the lack of moderation, but also that within us which prevents moderation: the inability to attune our actions so as to make them accordant and harmonious with a single purpose; the lack of ability to "govern, manage, or control" our lives according to a meaningful plan. An intemperate life is an untimed life, a life out of control.

I recall my first experience at auto mechanics as a boy working on an old 1915 model Ford engine. After days of immersion in grease, with my father's help I had tightened the bearings, ground the valves, and put in new piston rings. Finally I cranked it up. None of us will ever forget what happened. The motor started with all the noise one would ever want to hear—backfiring, coughing, and spitting. My dog was underneath the car sound asleep at the time. With the first backfire he came out from under and streaked off in the distance, yelping in sheer terror. After the excitement had died down, I got one of my friends who was a real mechanic to diagnose the trouble. What was the matter with the car? "Why," he said, "it's all out of time. The spark hits the cylinder head at the wrong time to explode the gas in the cylinder with the proper force. You'll have to put it back in time."

Like that ancient jalopy of mine, our world and many of our lives are sadly out of time and out of tune with reality. We have our desires hitting the cylinders of our actions at the wrong time and for the wrong purposes, and as a result our homes and our world are filled with discordant noise, weak and ineffective action, and terrifying threats of future calamity. We and our world are sadly out of joint with the good purpose of our Creator, and the only way we may learn how badly out of time we are is through the suffering we have already met and the threats of disaster posed by our power out of control. This is truly one of the most tragic symptoms of our Sin: the doing of good things but in the wrong time and spirit and with the wrong emphasis.

Blessed Are the Pure in Heart

We must have proper timing, integration, as the psychologists call it—the unification of our lives in such a way that things fit together and conflicts are removed. Self-love, as we have seen, is unable to provide this integration. Instead of centering our desires and passions, the result of self-love is to scatter and divide. One of the great gifts of the Spirit within us, writes Paul, is proper timing; the fruit of the Spirit is self-control, temperance. "For God did not give us a spirit of timidity but a spirit of power and love and self-control." (II Tim. 1:7.)

When Dante arrived at the sixth terrace in Purgatory, he found a tree hung with sweet-smelling fruit. Voices were heard from among the leaves recording examples of temperance—the fact that those whose lives are centered in the divine purpose and love have always possessed this self-control. As the angel came to erase the sixth sin mark, representing gluttony, from Dante's forehead, the heavenly choir sang:

> Blessed are they, whom grace
> Doth so illume, that appetite in them
> Exhaleth no inordinate desire,
> Still hungering as the rule of temperance wills.

Then as Dante moved on with lighter feet and hopeful heart to the seventh terrace, he saw the crowd of once noble and great souls burning in the fire of lust. Again he was depressed and in despair, but the angel of God again appeared:

> Joy was in his mien.
> Forth of the flame he stood upon the brink;
> And with a voice, whose lively clearness far
> Surpass'd our human, "Blessed are the pure
> In heart," he sang.

As Dante walked toward the fire, reluctantly, fearfully, he heard a voice from the other side "that sang, did guide us"; and following the voice,

> We issued forth,
> There where the path led upward. "Come," we heard,
> "Come, blessed of my Father."

178

The "pure in heart" who hear their Father's invitation are blessed because they are on center, balanced, integrated around one great love which harmonizes all their desires and gives them a unity of direction from which temperance and self-control are possible. A pure heart is a symbol of the depths of one's personality, including the affections and the will, when it is thus unified at center. Jesus used another expression to signify the same thing: "a single eye." "When your eye is sound [or single], your whole body is full of light; but when it is not sound [double], your body is full of darkness. Therefore be careful lest the light in you be darkness. If then your whole body is full of light, having no part dark, it will be wholly bright, as when a lamp with its rays gives you light." (Luke 11:34-36.) It was no coincidence that Jesus used the word "body" in this connection; "your whole body is full of light"—all its functions are bright and beautiful—when your eye is single. The enjoyment of physical pleasure and beauty becomes holy as a part of the blessings God intends for his children who are pure in heart.

"Purity of heart is to *will* one thing," writes Kirkegaard in the classic book of devotion *Purity of Heart*. His experience as a youth taught him the futility of attempting to live on the purely aesthetic level of haphazardly "rejecting the unpleasant and choosing only the pleasant." He was constantly embarrassed by the sense of ought and the demands of duty. In the company of brilliant aesthetes in Copenhagen, and with sufficient wealth to do what he pleased, he tried the way of pleasure for its own sake and found, as all others have found who have tried it, that it led straight to the despair which he called "sickness unto death." In his *Either/Or* is described the discovery, which is central in the redemption of any person, that one must choose either to live by immediately determined, spontaneous choices moment by moment, or to live by the long-term choices of the will which give him the perspective of "eternity in time." "Were he to surrender himself to the ethico-religious 'instant,' there would be no need to discard the aesthetic 'moment,' for there is no fundamental opposition between aesthetics and religion." [16] That is, when one is willing to do the will of God in every instant, including this one, he may in the right time enjoy the aesthetic moment as part of the will of God. "The art of mastering pleasure," writes Kierkegaard, "is not so much in annihilating it or entirely renouncing it, as in determining the instant" when it is to be put into effect. Only he who has completely surrendered his self-loving will to the eternally loving will of God can determine the instant when pleasure belongs.

Indeed, this necessity for timing is the whole secret not only of good morality, but of art and science as well. The difference in a child's discords at the piano and the great music of the master is not that some notes are good and some bad, but that all are bad when played out of time and harmony with the others, while all are good when played in time and harmony with the others. Thus also with art; there are not good and bad colors, or ugly and beautiful; but all colors are beautiful when blended in proper proportions. A skillful athlete is not only successful in the game but a delight to watch, because his timing is so perfect.

How Does One Get a Pure Heart?

Just as the musician wills one thing over a sufficient number of hours of practice and is thereby able to execute a difficult piece of music with the beauty of proper timing, so in the business of living one who is pure in heart begins to will one thing with the will of God. He continues to will one thing through conscious practice in prayer, meditation, fellowship, and action. He practices the fine art of living as a son of God and a member of the divine family. It is by the act of choosing, in which one surrenders all secondary choices to the love of God's good will for him and for all the human family, that one enters the kingdom of heavenly freedom to use and not abuse his body and the personalities of those about him. Kierkegaard uses a very strong word for "choice"—the word "leap" (German, "sprung"; Danish, "spring"). "The aesthete does not live," he says, because he does not "choose [leap with his will]

[16] T. H. Croxall, *Kierkegaard Studies* (Chicago: Alec R. Allenson, Inc., 1948).

180

before God." [17] This is the leap, or spring, of faith by which we choose to belong to our Father and to live in the spirit of Christ, which is the spirit of Christlike love. Kierkegaard is right in making it essentially an act of the will. True, our intellect and reason may be convinced, through a knowledge of the life and work of Jesus and of those who caught his Spirit, that God, the mighty Architect, has a plan for his universe and a plan for each of us. We may believe that "even the hairs of [our] head are all numbered" (Matt. 10:30) in the sense that the Father's loving purpose for us means *becoming* something, *doing* something, that is eternally valuable. But however strongly we are convinced intellectually of the truth of God in Christ, we still are not pure in heart, on center, until we have taken the leap of faith and chosen once and for all to live by that purpose and to accept the fellowship of the Spirit in the divine family.

To illustrate: An alcoholic came to his pastor, who had been counseling with him in previous weeks, with the despairing admission, "I believe I am going to die if I don't get a drink." The minister had been talking with him about the necessity of dying to the old self-love with its fantasies and pipe dreams. He had tried to help the poor victim of alcohol see that his insatiable thirst was a symptom of this old man, which must be crucified and killed (as Paul described the negative part of the leap of faith by which one enters the new relation with the Spirit of God in which self-control and temperance are possible). Now as his friend stood before him with the confession of being ready to die unless he could get a drink, the pastor said, "All right; go home and die!" The alcoholic was angry at first until he remembered the experience of Paul which his pastor had described. Without another word he turned and went to his room. A few days later he came back with a new light in his eyes. "I did what you said; I went home and died. Now for the first time I am beginning to be set free." And it was so. Surely this is the miracle that has taken place in thousands of drunkards who with the help of the Church and Alcoholics Anony-

---

[17] *Ibid.*

mous, have made the supreme choice or leap of faith. They have been able to lead sober lives in which for the first time in years they begin to enjoy life.

What was it that died within this alcoholic and that must die within each of us? It was misplaced self-love demanding the feeling within, even if evidence is lacking without, that we are important, big shots. It is only when I choose by a great leap of the will to accept my place in the love of God, when I see God's picture of my true self, which I want with all my heart, that I renounce this false self-picture. The same twelve steps which the alcoholic takes in the Alcoholics Anonymous method are necessary for the adulterer, the glutton, the self-righteous gossiper, or the person unable to control his temper or keep from being envious and avaricious. They are steps taken from the methods of every Christian evangelist since the beginning. The textbook *Alcoholics Anonymous* is recommended reading for any person who wants to be truly free, not just from alcohol, but from any other slavery of self-love. Two of these steps need especial emphasis here—the second and the twelfth. After admitting that one is helpless in his own power to overcome this habit and that there is One whose power is able to deliver him, he makes a "decision to turn my life over to God as I understand him." It is significant that most of the alcoholics who have found freedom from slavery to their false selves through the Alcoholics Anonymous program have been those with a fair Christian background: that is, who have been taught in their youth something of the love of the Father of our Lord Jesus Christ. Those who know little or nothing of the Christlike God have never been able, so far as I know, to find deliverance until they have been taught something of the nature of God as revealed in Christ. Sometimes, it is true, through the sheer power of the fellowship they get better for a time; but unless they understand and follow the spiritual part of the program, they soon lose even the value of the fellowship.

The twelfth step in the program is also of crucial importance. One thing all admit who have witnessed some of the victories won is that only those who take the twelfth step seriously ever get really well. This step declares the intention to help others thus ill by sharing with them their insights and by going to them when they are in need. A large part of the therapy of healing is the sense of belonging to a blessed fellowship where one is not blamed but accepted for what he is, where he is believed in, loved, and helped to a new life. Here is a church, whether it is thus called or not, in its most elemental form, where people who have been alienated and disinherited by family and community are once more accepted and made to feel a sense of belonging to one another. The twelfth step is *agape* love in action. If there is a power called God who loves me and cares for me, a poor drunken bum whom everyone else has abandoned, and shows his love to me through this wonderful group of friendly people, the least I can do is to show that same love to others. Hence the willingness of A.A.'s to sit up for hours with those whose acquaintance they have barely made as they help them get over a "fall." One is delivered from the pains of twisted self-love in all its manifestations only as he accepts his place in God's love and goes out to share this love with others. As was pointed out in Chapter III, it is the lack of such intimate fellowship in too many churches that robs the church of its rightful power in the redemption of its members.

We must die to self-love in order truly to live in the love of God. This does not mean that we die to our emotions, to our desires, or to our instincts, as those falsely believe who say, "I am not ready to commit myself to Christ, for I am unwilling to give up the fun of living." We must die to the false way of using these emotions, desires, and instincts. We must die to the false choice of the Gyntian Self, which blocks our emotions and keeps them from being free and going in the right channels. It is like the difference in a river flooded and out of control, running in torrents over homes and lands, destroying that which it touches, and the same river controlled by a huge dam, with its waters more beautiful than ever, but now turning great turbines to make electricity to light a large city and spilling over to be used in irrigation ditches to transform the desert into a garden. The same river, the same power, but redirected. That is the difference between human life with faith in Christ and without it. It requires the death of these things that are hurtful, these compulsions that twist and destroy our emotions or cause them to be blocked, to make possible the life of these same emotions turned into right channels. The same power, but beautiful rather than destructive.

"Always dying, yet behold I live!" This is the perennial experience of Christians who live more and more in the power and self-control of the Spirit. They are able to choose the highest good in the "instant" and to make a "sacrament of the present moment," as Pierre de Caussade calls it, and to enjoy the simple pleasures of the body when it is fitting to do so. Paul's emphasis on *always* dying needs to be remembered. One does not make the leap of faith just once and forevermore be exempted from choice. One chooses the supreme good for all instants in a given moment of time; but unless he continually reaffirms and leaps again and again by an act of the will, he will find himself slipping back into aestheticism and its deadening round of destructive futility. The first leap of faith may be a longer leap than any of the others, and more difficult; but the second and the third and the ten thousandth are equally important. "I die daily," is the way Paul describes this necessity. "I pommel my body and subdue it, lest after preaching [this freedom] to others I myself should be disqualified." (I Cor. 9:27.)

Freedom Through Discipline

Freedom in art, music, athletics, or science, or any other worthy endeavor, comes only to the disciplined. Is it any wonder that in the most difficult of all arts, the art of living in the power of the Holy Spirit, the liberty of the spirit comes only to the disciplined? Elton Trueblood clearly points out the fact that those spiritual movements which have resulted in large numbers of persons living redemptively have been those which emphasized disciplined living.[18]

We all want the fruits of the Spirit: peace, joy, contentment,

[18] *Alternative to Futility* (New York: Harper & Bros., 1948).

self-control. Who doesn't? But so few of us want the things that produce these fruits. We are like the little moron who rushed into the barbershop demanding a haircut but fast. "Well, all right, but take your hat off and sit down," said the barber. The little moron refused and once more excitedly demanded a haircut. "Why don't you take your hat off and sit down?" "Because," said the little fellow, "I'm in too big a hurry." If we are in too much of a hurry to do the things necessary to accept the gifts of the Spirit, which make everything fit in proper timing, we will continue to be slaves to self-love and its passions and appetites.

There are four disciplines which are musts for one who would be pure in heart with resulting liberty in the Spirit. They are: (1) the discipline of private prayer and meditation, which at best is a "pilgrimage from self to God"; (2) the discipline of regular worship, by which we set ourselves in a position of adoration, thanksgiving, confession, petition, and intercession before the Father in the company of the blessed fellowship; (3) the discipline of witnessing to the reality of the love of God in Christ in every way possible and to every person possible; and (4) the discipline of giving, by which we express love for the lost and least as well as the ones about us who have already accepted their places in the divine family.

None of these four disciplines are valuable when forced upon us from without as our Christian duty, or as the way to be considered righteous by others, or even for showing God how good we are. Only when they are the result of the Great Choice, the continuing expression of the leap of faith by which our wills day after day, hour after hour, are surrendering our minds and hearts to the influence of the Holy Spirit, only then are they the means of grace which lets the light in so that our bodies become full of brightness and life. We are to pray and worship, to give and serve, through the fellowship, not by mood or by whim, but with a steady purpose, reaffirmed each day, to relate our lives to the Spirit. This necessity for spiritual discipline has been well-nigh lost in our insistence on "freedom" in worship, which has become a shameful license to do as we please even in the noble disciplines of the Christian life. We pray and go to worship only when we feel like it. We give when it is convenient. When we witness—though we hardly ever do—it is not by a consistent, disciplined plan. This means that for multitudes of professing Christians prayer and worship are only for emergencies or special occasions and fall sadly short of the total surrender of life by which the spirit of freedom and life comes. We are creatures of spiritual whims; and no great power of self-control, much less of creative achievement, has ever yet been released by a whim. We will learn some day, even in tragic ineptitude and weakness, that one never attains the freedom of the Spirit who does not regularly and consistently and wholeheartedly practice the surrender of the spirit, and the acceptance and dedication of himself in prayer and worship, witnessing and giving, as a member of the blessed fellowship.

No one of us can integrate himself by his own wisdom and efforts. His Sin of self-love keeps him "riding the goat," forever thinking that now at last he is ready to enjoy life; but "though the fiends gave him hot lead to lap, his thirst is none the less." With the young actress in the moving picture *All About Eve* who had through costly struggle at last arrived at the top, we too will cry, "I have everything to make me happy, but I am so unhappy. Oh, you who know everything about so many things, tell me something about me!"

At last, like Dante, we step through the fire to a new level of loving. The fierce flames of self-love have been burning up our hopes and joys, but now at last we yield to the cooling, calming touch of the eternal love which puts out the fires that were slowly destroying us and leads us to the refreshing streams of purposeful, loving service. The sin mark of lust is removed from our brows, and we begin to have the greatest fun of our lives as we share in the redemptive love of the family of God. Now the simple joys of taste, sight, sound, smell, and feeling are part of the abundance which we can use when the instant is right without losing our joy or paling the joy of any other. Now we know the blessed freedom of Augustine, who said, "Love God with all your heart and soul

186

and mind and strength and do as you please." At last we are free to have fun as God's children without being slaves to our fun, and we are able to thrill to the joy of him whose magnificent purpose includes not only the joy of simple things, but the joy of love that "endured the cross, despising the shame, and is seated at the right hand of the throne of God" (Heb. 12:2).

"Blessed are the pure in heart, for they shall see God." They shall rejoice in the liberty of great living timed to the heartbeat of eternal love.

Chapter *VIII*

ANXIETY and WORRY

Into Productive Peace—Serenity with Concern

———————◆———————

Is THERE ANYWHERE IN ALL THIS UNIVERSE A PLACE OF SECURITY, a rock of refuge, a strong fortress, that cannot be shaken? Is man's life

> ...a dream in the night, a fear among fears,
> A naked runner lost in a storm of spears?

Must we always be torn between a bloated picture of ourselves as the lord and master of all we survey and a deflated picture of ourselves as the plaything of vast unconscious forces? Is there any deliverance from the deep-seated anxiety of failure, frustration, guilt, meaninglessness, despair, and death? If there is, no matter how cocky and self-assured we have been, there are times when most of us cry:

> Lead thou me
> to the rock that is higher than I.

"The beginning of wisdom is the acknowledgement of our creaturehood," wrote Maeterlinck. Anxiety—or worry, as it is popularly called—is the ultimate folly of a creature who refuses to acknowledge his creaturehood. It is the final symptom of the Sin of the man who plays God.

Creaturehood implies insecurity, inadequacy, mortality, finiteness, incompleteness. It means we are limited by time, space, physical weakness, disease, by our ignorance and lack of knowledge, and by the acts of others. But we long to be what only God can be: unlimited, timeless, powerful over all things, knowing everything, possessing everything. Human life on earth, however, is basically fragile and insecure. On this small planet, itself only an infinitesimal speck in the universe, man's life is possible only because of the preservation of a remarkable balance of gases in the air we breathe; of the distance between the sun, moon, and earth; of the speed with which the earth revolves; and by just enough and not too much or too little rainfall. The same frailty attaches to our physical bodies; how easily the balance between red and white corpuscles, hormones, acids in the stomach, and glandular secretions is upset.

There is a story of a little boy who asked his mother where we came from. She answered that we came from dust and would return to dust. A little later he called, "Mummy, come here quick!" She ran to the bedroom; and the little fellow, pointing under the bed, said, "There are a lot of people under there, but I can't tell whether they are coming or going." Whether coming or going, our lives are subject to the variations of a sometimes beneficent, sometimes destructive nature: earthquakes, tornadoes, excessive heat, floods. Our anxieties are increased by the insecurities of war, depression, disease, old age, and most of all by the deep-seated failures within each of us to achieve what we want to achieve, to reach the goals of our dreams, be they conscious or unconscious.

We are insecure, limited, finite—that is our fate.

We may be secure and creative in the love of the eternal Father— that is our opportunity.

We cannot remove our anxiety and insecurity—our attempt to do so is our Sin. When we try to guarantee our own security and the security of our loved ones and act as if we were infinite, unlimited, and immortal, we are "leaning against the wind." Call it pride or self-love or anything we like, this Sin, as has been shown, is the parent of all the destructive and crippling attitudes and acts.

We have traced the way in which this one Sin of man has resulted in the sins of conceit, vanity, envy, hate, jealousy, intolerance, anger, avarice, covetousness, lust, gluttony, dejection, and self-loathing. This last chapter deals with the final symptom of our Sin: abnormal anxiety and useless worry.

A distinction needs to be made between a proper anxiety, a normal concern, which is of the very essence of human creativity; and the fruitless, destructive anxiety which results from willful sin. "Anxiety, as a permanent concomitant of freedom, is thus both the source of creativity and a temptation to sin. It is the condition of the sailor, climbing the mast (to use a simile), with the abyss of the waves beneath him and the 'crow's nest' above him. He is anxious about both the end toward which he strives and the abyss of nothingness into which he may fall." [1] There is a healthy concern, resulting from our state of insecurity, which has produced most of our creative work. Under the spur of providing physical safety and plenty, progress in better and more dependable food, clothing, housing, communication, medicine, and surgery has been made. However, when through excessive fear of insecurity we dedicate too much of our time and energy to the quest for security, whether physical or psychic, life becomes unproductive; and that which was meant to be a spur to effort becomes a blockade on the road to achievement. Something like this is happening to millions of people today. A survey by *Fortune Magazine* among college students revealed that a sizeable portion of them were more interested in security than opportunity: "a cautious, subdued generation that will not stick its neck out. It keeps its shirt on . . . its chin up, and its mouth shut!" This is not a fair description of all youth of today, but it does describe many of them and their elders. One reason why statism, whether Communism or Fascism, is such a threat is that it promises security even at the price of liberty and millions are ready to buy it.

The abnormal anxiety which produces the neurotic search for security is grinding out personality maladjustments and breakdowns.

[1] Niebuhr, *op. cit.* Used by permission of Charles Scribner's Sons.

190

Children brought up in insecure homes, where such anxiety rules, are almost sure to grow up warped and twisted. Anxiety on the loose produces more and more tensions, hatreds, alcoholism, crimes, broken homes, and wars that wreck the normal security mankind could have. When we concentrate on security, then it is that we are most insecure. We upend the purposes of creation and cancel our true creativeness. We are made so that we need a measure of insecurity, incompleteness, and dissatisfaction to keep us growing and achieving; but unless at the same time we find a deep inner security by which our costly anxieties and worries are removed, we destroy all possibilities of growth. Tensions and struggles are good for us so long as they don't get inside of us. "All the water in the world can't sink a ship, so long as it doesn't get inside." Many human ships are leaking badly.

What! Worry a Sin?

That worry, as I shall call this symptom of our Sin, deserves the place of importance at the conclusion of the list of the seven deadly sins is obvious to every doctor, lawyer, judge, counselor, minister, or close observer who has seen the destructiveness and hurt caused by it. "This Age of Anxiety" is the appropriate name given to our time by W. H. Auden. By far the most popular books, bought by millions of people, are those with such titles as *Peace of Mind, How to Stop Worrying and Start Living, Peace of Soul, The Power of Positive Thinking, A Guide to Confident Living,* and *Beyond Anxiety.*[2] Evidently the sin of worry is more widespread than the other symptoms of man's Sin. Not all are envious, or lustful, or avaricious, or angry, or dejected; but most of us are at some time at least victims of useless and destructive anxiety. The symptom is found not only in atheists and agnostics, but in professing Christians. How seldom do we find persons with the serenity of the good woman who said, "When I work, I work hard; when I sit, I sit loose; and when I begin to worry, I go to sleep."

[2] The authors are respectively: Joshua Liebman, Dale Carnegie, Fulton Sheen, Norman Vincent Peale, James A. Pike.

191

Judge a tree by its fruits. Measure the evil of worry by the man-hours lost from work, by the joy-hours lost from living, by the health-hours lost from our years, by the great possibilities of good it destroys, and the misery it brings. Worry has probably done as much harm as the more obvious evils of stealing, lying, murder, and adultery. Back of most of these sins is not only man's prideful self-love, but his anxious attempts to remove his worries in his own way.

Worry is deceptive. It never comes in the guise of evil, but always appears to be a virtue, even more than other sins. The person who worries thinks he is doing a good thing. "I worry about you all the time—doesn't that show how much I love you?" Not at all. Anxiety over another person doesn't necessarily prove your love for that person. It may indicate your possessive self-love, the fear of your own loss. Worry is abnormal concern. It is concern that occupies the mind long after it can be put to any constructive use, and as such it is the most deceptive of evils. It slips around on our blind side—especially those of us who profess faith in God—and destroys us before we know it. It is an inverted or perverted virtue. It is the most futile dissipation possible. It is idiotic to spend hours turning over and over in our minds something which we cannot help, while our glands needlessly pump adrenalin into our blood further unfitting us to meet the situation as it is.

Why Worry?

The answer is simple: Because in our present condition we cannot help it. Seeking to save our own self-picture of life, we are threatened by the shadows that circumvent and thwart the rainbows of our ego-vision. It is therefore unrealistic and cruel for a minister, or doctor, or friend, to say, "All you need to do is to stop worrying." We cannot keep from being abnormally anxious any more than we can keep the wind from blowing by shaking our fists at it. The desperate feelings of inadequacy, apprehension, guilt, frustration, impotency, meaninglessness, and fear—part or all of which cause our worry no matter what the external reason assigned to it—cannot be done away by snapping the fingers. We may know why we are anxious and afraid, but that does not remove the worry.

With such universal awareness of the costliness of our anxieties, it is natural that a flood of books and articles have appeared giving various systems or techniques by which man can rid himself of the demon worry. Some have been simple, such as the Coué method of repeating many times a day: "Every day in every way I am getting better and better." Some have been complex combinations of self-psychiatry and metaphysics.[3] Some have contained helpful insights that have been received eagerly by millions of discouraged readers. Much of this mad scramble for serenity has been false and illusory because it has been based on two false ideas. One says: Tell yourself over and over that your troubles and sufferings and those of your fellow man are unreal—they exist only in your mind. If you just quit thinking about them, relax and think positively instead, you will escape all the pain and suffering. You will have peace of mind. The other false approach to our problem says: Admit evil and pain are real, but believe God is with you and therefore nothing bad can happen to you. If it works, you will be an exception. This method is based on isolated passages of scripture such as

> He will give his angels charge of you . . .
> no evil shall befall you;

but its adherents forget Jesus' rebuke to the tempter, who urged him to jump off the temple and be one of God's favorites, exempted from his physical laws: "You shall not tempt the Lord your God" (Matt. 4:7). Later, as Jesus himself met the anxious hours before his crucifixion, he reminded the disciples, "In the world you have tribulation; but be of good cheer, I have overcome the world" (John 16: 33).

Though containing elements of truth, both of these methods on the whole are false. They may give us a temporary security and peace of mind, but soon the crashing storms of life sweep over us,

[3] E.g., L. Ron Hubbard, *Dianetics* (New York: Hermitage House, Inc., 1950).

and we discover that pain and suffering are real and that God does not make an exception even of us.

Can We Possess Serenity with Concern?

Many of these methods of gaining peace of mind fall short because they overlook the necessity for a proper balance between serenity and concern, and because they expect either too much of man without God or too much of God without man.

I have pointed out how concern without serenity is slow but sure destruction of our health and well-being, as well as of our ability to be a positive part of mankind's redemption. We are victims of the pressures peculiar to modern life as well as the perennial tensions that have afflicted men in all ages. On the other hand, serenity without concern is the ultimate sin of self-centered people who have become callous and hardhearted. They are so immune to the pain and wrongs about them that they are able to say, "Aw, what the heck!" or, "Really, I couldn't care less!" [4]

Even many professedly religious people try to use faith in God as an opiate to deaden their concern and to give them peace of mind while doing and caring little or nothing about the trouble and suffering of their fellows. The gospel of relaxation may sound good to those who would avoid the Cross, but it has a hollow ring in a realistic world where the only true peace is always the result of struggle and difficulty. He who said, "My peace I give to you" (John 14:27), was also the one who said, "If any man would come after me, let him deny himself and take up his cross and follow me" (Mark 8:34). We cannot have his peace without his Cross. If we think we can, we will have to hear his other words that startled the smugness of the "good" people of his day who used their righteousness to build up a false peace: "I have not come to bring [this kind of] peace," he cried, "but a sword" (Matt. 10:34). Creative living demands the possession of true peace, which is serenity with concern.

Is productive peace possible in a world like this regardless of

---

[4] The sin of *accidia* or sloth—see Chapter V.

one's circumstances? Undoubtedly a deep serenity coupled with a passionate concern was the shining possession of Paul and the early Christians, as it has been of every person since who had a vital faith. This is not speculation, but the undisputed fact of history, past and present. Skeptics may question the source of this creative peace, but none can question its reality. The early Christians had such loving peace that thousands suffered and died without fear, "rejoicing that they were counted worthy to suffer dishonor for the name" (Acts 5:41). They had what all men wanted —an inner security which nothing could shake. Paul knew it in his own life. Writing to Timothy about one of his most difficult experiences, probaby in Ephesus, he says he "fought with beasts" (I Cor. 15:32). He testifies, "At my first defense no one took my part. . . . But the Lord stood by me and gave me strength" (II Tim. 4:16-17). He wrote to the Corinthians:

This priceless treasure we hold, so to speak, in a common earthenware jar—to show that the splendid power of it belongs to God and not to us. We are handicapped on all sides but we are never frustrated: we are puzzled, but never in despair. We are persecuted, but we never have to stand it alone: we may be knocked down but we are never knocked out, . . . always "going through it" yet never "going under." . . . We are penniless, and yet in reality we have everything worth having.

Here is God's answer to the anxieties of man's frailty, frustrations, and fears: "For it is the God who said, 'Let light shine out of darkness,' who has shone in our hearts to give the light of the knowledge of the glory of God in the face of Christ" (II Cor. 4:6). Vital Christianity may be described as loving serenity with Christlike concern—the concern of a great love and the serenity of a great peace, both resting on the divine love shining in the face of Jesus Christ. The result is patience, plus courage, added to fortitude.

The New Testament and other Christian writers are pretty plain about the possession of this peace or the lack of it. "For all who are led by the Spirit of God are sons of God. . . . Any one who does not have the Spirit of Christ does not belong to him." (Rom.

195

8:14, 9.) Now that is bitter medicine for those who consider themselves active Christians but who have Sin's symptom of hurtful
anxiety and fretful worry and are unable to get over it. Nevertheless,
said Paul, without the consciousness that you are a son of God you
will slip back into the same old slavish spirit of fear; but when you
are willing to say with genuine commitment of faith, "Abba!
Father!" the Spirit will bear witness with your spirit that you are a
child of God (Rom. 8:15-16). "The immediate consequence" of
this witness of the Spirit, declared John Wesley, "will be the fruit
of the Spirit, even 'love, joy, peace, long-suffering, gentleness, goodness, fidelity, meekness, temperance.' "

What then shall we say to this? If God is for us, who is against us?
He who did not spare his own Son but gave him up for us all, will he
not also give us all things with him? . . . Who shall separate us from the
love of Christ? Shall tribulation, or distress, or persecution, or famine, or
nakedness, or peril, or sword? . . . No, in all these things we are more than
conquerors through him who loved us. For I am sure that neither death,
nor life, nor angels, nor principalities, nor things present, nor things to
come, nor powers, nor height, nor depth, nor anything else in all creation, will be able to separate us from the love of God in Christ Jesus
our Lord. (Rom. 8:31-32, 35, 37-39.)

That is the reason, cried Paul, why we never collapse. "The
outward man does indeed suffer wear and tear, but every day the
inward man receives fresh strength. . . . This makes us confident
whatever happens." (II Cor. 4:16-17.) [5] The realism of the Christian
faith is a remarkable thing. It does not say we are to have a mind
in which there is nothing but sweetness and light or that we never
fall. It says: We are knocked down often, but never knocked out.
We never stay down. We may lose our serenity momentarily, as
Jesus did on the cross when he cried, "My God, why hast thou
forsaken me?" He was like us, for he, too, felt the pressure. But
like him we come back to say, "Father, into thy hands I commit
my spirit!" What Christian faith says is this: We may be handi-

[5] Phillips, *op. cit.*

196

capped on all sides, but never frustrated; puzzled, but never in despair. We will have tribulations, but be of good cheer; we serve one who will enable us to overcome. Had the early Christians not possessed this loving serenity, we would never have heard of Christianity and its God. Through two thousand years in those who have had faith the reality of the Spirit has shone through the darkness of men's folly and evil.

This is the testimony of thousands for whom loving, Christlike peace is a growing experience: serenity with concern comes through faith in God—it is the gift of his Spirit. "To believe in God," observed the Spanish Christian Miguel Unamuno, "is to desire his existence and to act as though he existed."

A care-worn mother prayed with her little girl at the close of the day. When they had concluded, the mother rose and immediately resumed an attitude of worried anxiety. The child looked up into her troubled face. "Why, Mother," she said, "you have just prayed!" "Yes, I know," the mother replied. Her small daughter answered simply, "I would think you could either worry or pray, but you couldn't do both." The wisdom of this little child beautifully describes the wisdom of the Christian faith in regard to worry. Without faith in the Christlike God as the source and sustainer of all things, who holds the keys to life's enigmas, we simply cannot conquer our anxieties. Our worry is the clearest indication of unbelief, and unbelief cuts us adrift from our true destiny and our greatest resources. If you are immersed in worry over things you cannot help or change, it is obvious you do not at that time believe in God. If you worry, you do not at that time trust. If you trust, you do not at the time of your trust worry. Either we seek to guarantee our own securities and to overcome our creaturely anxieties in our own way, or we surrender in complete trust and confident adoration and accept in that moment, even in the midst of life's worst tension, his gift of peace and serenity, as well as of love and concern.

"The fear of the Lord, that is wisdom" (Job 28:28), is the way Job described this double truth. Recognizing myself as a creature and accepting my rightful place as a created being rather than trying to act as the Creator puts in me a rightful fear of the Lord, who is the Creator. Whether or not this fear is destructive or productive then depends on the character of the creator Lord. If I believe the Lord is some grim monster or vast unconscious force, I am torn by a double anxiety of meaninglessness and frustration added to my fear of the future unknown. If, on the other hand, I commit my life to the faith that the Lord is the spirit of Christ, then the fear of the Lord becomes awe-filled trust, confident adoration, and loving attentiveness. Christian faith is a mixture of respect, admiration, awe, and love. Such fear is the beginning of wisdom, for it completely removes the abnormal, neurotic fears of the man within me who plays God. It joins my little powers to the creative powers of the Lord of heaven and earth, so that I am able to be a cocreator, a fellow worker with God (1 Cor. 3:9). Then I can say:

> At the heart of the cyclone tearing the sky
> And flinging the clouds and the towers by,
> Is a place of central calm;
> So here in the roar of mortal things,
> I have a place where my spirit sings,
> In the hollow of God's palm! [6]

This is not just poetry, but a wondrous fact. When we are sure of God—sure that this universe belongs to him and that it is never going to be snatched from his hands, sure that nothing can ever defeat him and that he is concerned about us and all his created children with the love of an eternal Father—we will overcome worry, and not until then.

How Can We Be Sure of God?

How can one be sure of God, the unseen, the infinite, the incomprehensible? God has shined through our darkness "to give the light of the knowledge of the glory of God in the face of Christ" (II Cor. 4:6). In him God is no longer the incomprehensible. Not

[6] Edwin Markham, "The Place of Peace." Reprinted by permission.

198

that we claim to comprehend or encompass all there is of God. He is still the infinite one, but he is no longer the totally unseen. That which we have seen and heard and which our hands have handled of the Word of life have we declared to you. (I John 1: 1-3.) On this fact Christians unalterably stand. Not only have we seen his glory shining in history in the face of Jesus Christ and in those who have followed him, but we have the witness of the "Spirit himself bearing witness with our spirit that we are children of God" (Rom. 8:16).

"An assurance was given me . . ." writes John Wesley of the experience which represented the turning point in his life. For thirty-five years he had struggled with his anxieties and insecurities. He had been worried about many things. He was seeking methodically, sometimes desperately, to save himself in another age of rationalism; but he could not be sure of the reality of God's forgiving love. Like modern man he doubted the character of the power behind all things. He was worried about his salvation and the state of his health. He was worried about what other people said or thought. On board ship, going to America as a missionary, Wesley became thoroughly frightened during a storm. He was amazed to see a group of Moravians in one corner of the ship praying and singing together, calm and unafraid. He describes what followed:

In the midst of the psalm . . . the sea broke over, split the mainsail in pieces, covered the ship, and poured in between the decks, as if the great deep had already swallowed us up. A terrible screaming began among the English. The Germans . . . calmly sang on. I asked one of them afterwards, "Was you not afraid?" He answered, "I thank God, no." I asked, "But were not your women and children afraid?" He replied mildly, "No, our women and children are not afraid to die."

Wesley knew he did not have that kind of faith. "I have a sin of fear," he wrote. When asked by the Moravian leader if he had the witness of the Spirit in his own life, he answered, "I do"; but in his diary he wrote, "I fear they were vain words!" Some years of increasing failure and frustration elapsed before Wesley sat one night in the little meeting of Moravians in Aldersgate Street, London, and found the witness of the Spirit which destroyed his anxious insecurity and made him forget himself. "An assurance was given me . . ." he writes of that great hour.

Obviously such blessed assurance of the reality of God in Christ is the focal need of our anxious, distraught lives. But how does one find God and be sure of him? What happened to Wesley at Aldersgate to transform his self-centered anxiety into such Christ-like concern? He was sure of God, but how did it happen, and why?

The answer to this question is a large one. Assurance, like love, is a gift of the Spirit in response to our faith. All that has been said in this book up to this point was meant to be relevant to the answer we need. The remainder of this chapter, however, is intended to be more than a summary of what has gone before. We need to deal with the question of the immediacy of the Spirit with our spirits. Call it mysticism or what you will, without this "practice of the Presence," which true prayer and worship can give, there can be no real assurance in us such as Paul, Wesley, and other victorious spirits in every age have possessed.

Our biggest difficulty, as it was for them, is our stubborn insistence on seeing or feeling God, or reasoning the whole thing out with logical exactness. This again is a symptom of our Sin—the attempt to escape the limitations of creaturehood. The first step in fulfilling the conditions of faith by which the gift of assurance comes is, therefore, the surrender of our demands for certain kinds of proof (intellectual, emotional, or physical) and the willingness to live by faith in him who is incomprehensible (infinitely beyond our powers of understanding) and yet immediate and near to us in the Holy Spirit. This does not mean the abdication of reason and selfhood, but using the highest faculties of mind and of selfhood.

The Mystery of the Incomprehensible

First, we must admit that all of life is a mystery. Death is a mystery. Birth is a mystery. Love is a mystery. And God is the deepest of all mysteries. The greatest things of life are among the incomprehensibles, as Albert Einstein calls them: that is, things that cannot be measured with the tools of science and that can neither be proved nor disproved. This does not mean that they are not objectively real, but that they can be only subjectively experienced; and it is our experience of them that makes us have faith that they are objectively real. For instance, says Einstein, here is the deep faith which scientists have in the "rationality of nature," which cannot actually be measured or demonstrated by science, but which is the basic assumption upon which all science rests.[7]

Even the Newtonian formula itself is not strictly valid, says one scientist.[8] That is, there are some facts that do not fit in; but our faith in the existence of such relationships is not destroyed because we cannot logically or conclusively prove it—we hope to find an even better formula to express it. It was just such a simple formula which Einstein advanced early in the century, but which was not given validation in the experience of scientists until the observations by Eddington's party on the solar eclipse of May 19, 1919. During this eclipse it was found that the "rays of the stars were deflected in passing by the sun to the precise extent formulated by Einstein." This does not mean, however, that Einstein's theory of relativity has exhausted the truth about the universe, but only that a small part of the mystery has been cleared. How has even this tiny bit of the mystery become known? Through the scientists' faith that nature is dependable, that there is a "certain correlation between nature and the human mind. This correlation has been described for hundreds and thousands of years by saying that the world has been created by a mind which has some properties of the human mind although it is much superior." [9]

It is upon this simple elemental faith that true religion as well as

[7] Philipp Frank, *Relativity: A Richer Truth* (Boston: Beacon Press, 1950).
[8] The Newtonian formula declares that the "entire seemingly incalculable complexity of the courses of the planetary bodies is governed with the help of the simple mathematical function $1/r_2$."
[9] Frank, *op. cit.* Used by permission of the Beacon Press.

true science rests. There is that in the supreme Mind which corresponds to something in the mind of the creature called man by which they can meet and understand and have communion with each other. To quote Einstein's own words:

> The most beautiful emotion we can experience is the mystical. It is the sower of all true art and science. He to whom this emotion is a stranger, who can no longer wonder and stand rapt in awe, is as good as dead. *To know that what is impenetrable to us really exists, manifesting itself as the highest wisdom and the most radiant beauty, which our full faculties can comprehend only in their most primitive forms—this knowledge, this feeling is at the center of true religiousness.* In this sense, and in this sense only, I belong to the ranks of devoutly religious men.[10]

Here is the only sure ground on which any truly religious man can stand: Humbly devoid of all pride in his own mind or knowledge, yet believing that what is impenetrable to us in its total reality really exists and that in the religious experience of mankind there is a vital clue to the nature of this supreme Mind.

In this sense the faith of a true scientist is the faith of a truly religious man. As scientists considering the nature of our universe, we have faith that our simple formulas are based on reality because they give us open doors to the strength and power and life that are in the universe. However, a true scientist does not become proud and take to himself the glory of being the master of the universe, or even believe that his simple formulas are the last word. To do so is pseudo science, or scientism, which is one of the most devastating symptoms of man's Sin.

Likewise, when as Christians we consider the nature of God, we have faith that in Christ Jesus and in communion with his Spirit we have a clue that is grounded in the gracious reality of the mighty God. Why do we believe it? Because this blessed relationship for countless thousands in every age has opened doors to new wisdom, new courage, new power, and new life which have never been

[10] *Ibid.*

202

known in any other way. Again, this relationship is lost and its power shorn when we begin to boast in prideful glory and to assume that we know all about God and that we are his special favorites. This is the sin of religion gone sour—attempting to use God for our own glory and convenience. The first step in religious assurance is to renounce this pride and to recognize that "now we see in a mirror dimly. . . . Now I know in part; then I shall understand fully, even as I have been fully understood." (I Cor. 13:12.)

This is the sublime faith that leads to an experience of God, so that we cry, "It was not I that found God, but I was found of him." The phrases "son of God," "in Christ," "filled with the Spirit," "God the Father, Son, and Holy Spirit," are all symbols of a reality which they represent but do not by any means describe. When we are possessed by the faith that now, in this moment, we are in the presence of the divine reality which is the most radiant beauty and the highest wisdom and the most gracious love, in whom "we live and move and have our being"; who "has borne our griefs and carried our sorrows; . . . was wounded for our transgressions, . . . bruised for our iniquities; . . . and with his stripes we are healed," then it is we too shall shout with the multitude which no man can number: "Hallelujah! For the Lord our God the almighty reigns. Let us rejoice and exult and give him the glory, Hallelujah! Salvation and glory and power belong to our God, for his judgments are true and just; and he shall reign for ever and ever! Amen! Hallelujah!" Then it is, and only then, that we will cease our petty strivings for self-exaltation and clamoring after things that leave us hollow men, emptier and thirstier each hour and each day than we were the hour and the day before. We will lose our deep-seated anxieties as life becomes an ever-increasing opportunity for glorifying our Lord and enjoying him forever.

Faith Without Proof?

Our difficulty is in making our commitment to accept this reality by faith without the emotional, logical proofs our insecurity craves.

Even though it is true that in the physical world we accept a thousand things by faith every day, from the purity of the water we drink to the radio and television waves we experience, in the spiritual world we disregard the abundant evidence in the experience of millions of people and demand some kind of tangible proof. "Show us the Father [we want to see God], and we shall be satisfied" (John 14:8), said Philip to Jesus in their last hour together. John Wesley also had this trouble. "I want a faith that one cannot have without knowing that he hath it," he said. A worthy desire, but what Wesley really wanted was not faith; he wanted to see God or feel him in some overwhelming fashion so he wouldn't need faith. Many of us are like that. If we could be overwhelmed by God, knocked down with a blinding light as happened to Paul, we would believe. That is, we want to gamble on a sure thing; we do not want to act on faith.

The Pharisees had given the same excuse for their refusal to believe in Jesus. Show us a sign! they cried. A few falling stars or some unusual miracles will do, but we want proof before we surrender our position. Jesus answered significantly, "An evil and adulterous generation seeks for a sign" (Matt. 12:39).

Why must we have faith? Why doesn't God overwhelm us with the proof of his existence and character? Jesus answered when he refused in his second temptation to throw himself down from the temple and to tempt God to give such a sign. Jesus knew the state of mind of the people who would witness such an exhibition. He knew they would fall down and worship him, not out of love but out of fear. He refused the temptation, saying (if I may paraphrase his words), "Thou shalt not tempt the Lord to change his ways with me, to destroy man's freedom. God does not want slaves, but sons." (Matt. 4:7.) God is hidden from the casual observer because were he to reveal himself in even a small part of his full glory and power, no man could stand it. Everybody would obey him as a trembling slave obeys a master with a whip in his hand. There would be no choice in life between good and evil if God, who is behind the good, stood over us with a cosmic whip. We will find God, therefore, only as we recognize him by faith in his revelation in Jesus Christ and in those who have caught his spirit.

An obscure saint in the Middle Ages was making this same mistake. He had been praying hour after hour for a realization of God's presence. "Oh, if I only knew!" he wailed. "Oh, if I only knew!" At last, when he was spent, a voice within him said, "What would you do if you most certainly knew? Do now what you would do then and rest secure." That is the secret. *Act on your belief in God, and you will know.* This acting on faith does not mean a blind acceptance of untruth, "believing what you know ain't so," as a little boy put it. It does not mean doing what the mad queen counseled Alice in Wonderland, who was having difficulty believing some of the incredible things in the strange world underneath, to take a deep breath, and believe anyhow. "Faith is not belief in spite of evidence, but life in scorn of consequence," said Kirsopp Lake. We have so many evidences of God—in the beauty all about us, in the love of our dear ones, in the human experience of sacrifice, and supremely in Christ. "Believe me that I am in the Father and the Father in me," said Jesus to his disciples; "or else believe me for the sake of the works themselves" (John 14:11) —but believe. There are many evidences of the reality of the Christlike God, but only those who are willing to act by faith on the evidences of God in human experience will ever find him in their own experiences.

What happened to Wesley at Aldersgate? At least this much is evident: he gave up in that hour his attempt to guarantee his own security and to be sure of God by the particular kind of feeling or demonstrable proof which he had heretofore demanded. He surrendered himself by faith to accept the forgiveness and love of God as revealed in Christ. The assurance of God came to him *after* he had given up his demand for his own kind of assurance. Christian assurance, wrote Wesley, is

strictly speaking . . . a conclusion drawn partly from the Word of God and partly from our own experience. The Word of God says everyone who has the fruit of the Spirit is the child of God; experience, or inward consciousness, tells me that I have the fruit of the Spirit . . . therefore, I am a child of God. . . . The true witness of the Spirit is known by its fruit, "love, peace, joy"; not indeed preceding, but following it!

Later in life Wesley wrote, "I could no more worry than I could curse or swear." And among his last words as, surrounded by his preachers, he departed this life were, "The best of all is, God is with us." John Wesley was sure of God. He was sure of God because he had committed himself by faith to serve his Christ, even though he could not see or feel him as he had longed to do.

"If with All Your Hearts You Truly Seek Me . . ."

The second condition required for a faith resulting in the gift of serenity with loving concern is a determination to seek for God until we find him in conscious communion. Faith is a gift; but before anyone receives it, he has to want it as the central desire of his life—want it enough to take the time to fulfill the conditions of accepting it. There will have to be the first time, whether you *feel* like it or not, when you decide to cast your life in the balance on the side of your conviction that there is at the heart of all things a God who is like Jesus. You must decide that you are from that moment on going to think and live by that conviction. You do not then *have* faith as a completed thing; you only *begin* to have faith. You may lose it the next hour or the next day, as the old prideful longings come back to take control. Finding the assurance of God which transforms anxiety and makes patient, steadfast, courageous concern possible is, therefore, a process of *continually reaffirming our determination to live* by our conviction. It is by loving attentiveness and awe-filled adoration, as we commune with the Spirit, that the unconscious mind is brought more and more under the influence of the major conviction of our lives. "Ask, and it will be given you; seek . . . ; knock, and it will be opened to you. . . . Blessed are those who hunger and thirst [after God], for they shall be satisfied. . . . Blessed are the pure in heart, for they shall see God." (Luke 11:9; Matt. 5:6, 8.) " 'If with all your hearts you truly seek me, you shall ever truly find me!' thus said the Lord."

The big trouble with most of us—and we might as well confess it—is that we do not really want God; our hearts are impure, double-minded. We want God, but we also want a dozen other things equally as much. We feel it is up to us to guarantee our own security and the security of our loved ones. We are really afraid of God, as Adam was—afraid we will lose some of these things so dear to us—so we hide from him. We are like the student who answered, when confronted with the challenge of Christ's call, "I don't want to be great; I want to be comfortable." We want to be comfortable, or popular, or rich, to have fun in our own way, to be famous. A deep part of us wants to find the greatness of life's meaning, to be free, to be sure of God; but the other part of us is afraid if we find God, he might get in our way. And thus even many professing Christians never find the assurance of God that sets them free. God to millions of people is an inconvenience. If only they could forget him, how much easier it would be. They have just enough faith to make them miserable, but not enough to give them serenity with concern.

There is an old Indian tale of a student walking disconsolately in a garden when he met an old man dressed in a saffron robe and sitting by a pond. Seeing the perplexed look on the young man's face, the old sage asked, "What is it you seek?" The discouraged young man answered, "I'm seeking for God. Can you tell me where I might find him?" The old man assured him that he could and, rising, led the youth by the hand into the pool. When they were about neck-deep in the water, the old man suddenly seized the student by the neck and pushed him under. He held him there until the youth thought surely he would drown. At last he came up, sputtering and coughing the water from his lungs. The old man led him back to the side of the pool and sat down. "How does that help me find God?" the student asked indignantly. "What did you want most under the water?" inquired the sage. "Air. I wanted air more than all else," answered the student. The old man took him again by the hand and said, "When you want God as you then wanted air, you will find him."

Blessed are they who hunger and thirst after God and his rightness; they shall be fully satisfied.

There is a third and last condition of the faith that makes us sure of God: You and I will find God when we want him with enough devotion to be willing to surrender our self-picture of life to him and to trust him without reservation. This is the only way we will be able to be rid of the pagan attempt to use God to give us peace and safety in our own way. Our faith becomes an action of trust in which we let ourselves be used by God for the eternally worth-while purposes that never know defeat. "If any man's will is to do his will, he shall know. . . ." (John 7:17.)

John Wesley was a different person after his Aldersgate experience, for in that hour he had surrendered his self-picture of life without reservation. Years later someone asked him how he knew he had found God. He must have smiled to himself as he thought of the difference in his life then and before Aldersgate. Before, everything had gone wrong; he was filled with conflicts, doubts, worry. He was easily discouraged, afraid; he had failed life's central tests. Since Aldersgate he had forgotten himself, and his once-strong demand for comfort and interesting friends was no longer important. He had surrendered also his demands for an overwhelming emotional experience, or logical proof, and was willing to trust God even if he didn't have the feeling he thought he ought to have. Regardless of what happened, he was now going to do God's will as he trusted in Christ. And what a difference it made! He now had not only a warm heart, but a life that was on fire. Before, he had driven people away; now he preached to twenty thousand people on the hillside, each one thinking he was speaking to him. He was so sure of God that through him, and those who had his Spirit, there began the great spiritual awakening that saved England from a bloody revolution. In answer to the man's question Wesley said, in effect, "You can be sure of God when you have the fruits of the Spirit: love, hope, peace, patience, kindness, self-control."

Are you willing to trust God without reservation when it comes to your fun and pleasure, your health, your future, your vocation, your desire for recognition and popularity, your loved ones, your longing for security—with your life itself? Until you are, there is no chance whatever that you will find the serenity of a loving concern in your relations with God.

As a self-sufficient person trying to play God one would have to say, "I must have fun just the way I want it. I couldn't trust God here. Some day when I am old, but not now." But as described in the preceding chapter, the experience of millions declares, "Surrender your demand for pleasure just the way you want it, commit yourself to a loving concern, and you will find true pleasure and more fun than you ever knew." The fruit of the Spirit is also joy.

Surrender your health to him, and you will find real health. There is a certain woman in a west Texas city who used to be an invalid. From her youth she had wanted health more than anything else; but the more she desired it, the less she seemed to have. She became an anxiety-ridden invalid, filled with resentment and self-pity, a burden to herself and those about her. One day she picked up a New Testament and read the words of Jesus about seeking to save one's life and losing it. Suddenly it dawned on her what she had been doing, and she exclaimed, "That's it! I've been seeking desperately to save my health, and I've been losing it, and life, too." That moment she surrendered her health to God. "Even if I am an invalid the rest of my life, I am willing to see the good you are bringing me and to make the most of each hour and each day." She regained her health and became one of the most creative and beloved women in the community, whose Christlike concern for others was matched by her sweet serenity. She was well physically, but first of all she had become well within. She would have continued well within even if she had remained an invalid.

The same thing happened to Job, when sitting on an ash heap, covered with boils, condemned by his friends and his wife, there came a time when he surrendered his rebellion against God over his condition. He knew he had not been perfect, but he had not sinned enough to deserve all the suffering he had experienced. At first he wanted to come into the presence of God only so that he could argue with him, but at last he quit asking why, and with a great commitment of faith he cried, "I know that my Redeemer lives. . . . He knows the way that I take; when he has tried me, I shall come forth as gold." (Job 19:25; 23:10.) It was only then that God made himself known to Job, and his clamorings stopped. Notice that Job did not get the answer to his question: Why this suffering? The Book of Job doesn't tell why people suffer; but it does say that when we trust God, we find him, and then the question of suffering does not matter. When Job trusted without reservation, he found God and his health returned. But even if he had remained covered with boils, he would have been well.

The Dread of Death

Surrender your demand for security of a certain kind and you will find real security which no one, nor any circumstance—not even death—can disturb. There is a security belonging to those who live in our Father's house which even the loss of one's earthly habitation cannot touch. "Let not your hearts be troubled; [have faith] in God. . . . In my Father's house are many rooms."

The anxiety of death is universal and inescapable. It underlies and colors far more of our thinking and acting than most of us would admit. There is something within us which resists and resents the thought of the "complete loss of self which biological extinction implies."

It is one of the most interesting facts of history that Christians who have been sure of God in Christ not only have outlived but have outdied the pagan world, as T. R. Glover has so aptly put it. As illustrated by Stephen, who cried, "I see Jesus!" as he died with the stones pelting his brow, and by the thousands dying in the arena or burning at the stake, it is a fact that those with faith in Christ have conquered the fear of death. "Death is swallowed up in victory" (I Cor. 16:54), cried Paul. Not only physical death, but death in life, including the fear of death. The anxiety of meaninglessness and of guilt is the sting of death. When these are removed, the spirit of perpetual youth belongs to our hearts and death has lost its sting.

The sustained conviction of a future life that is infinitely desirable is possible only to those with a living faith in Christ through whom they know a rich companionship in the Spirit. Mere continued existence is not to be sought, in fact is to be abhorred. Why should anyone desire to continue an existence that has grown stale, unprofitable, from which even in this life he has attempted to escape? Only those who have found eternal life in time, as they enjoy the fruits of the Spirit, may truly desire it for eternity. Faith in a future life rests on our faith in the character of God—whether or not we truly believe that

> The Power that holds the planets in their courses,
> That places limits on the restless sea,
> Holds my life too within its mighty keeping
>   Always holds me.
>
> I say this over and over when storms are heavy,
> I say it when the night is on the land.
> I whisper that behind the Power Almighty
>   Is God's kind hand.
>
> And so I rest as a man rests on the river,
> Quiet and calm amid life's troubled flow,
> I know I am held by a Power and a Love
>   That never will let go.[11]

Such faith is the final security. It belongs to him who acts upon his conviction of the ever-present reality of the Christ Spirit,

> that behind the Power Almighty
> Is God's kind hand.
>
> .   .   .   .
>
> a Power and a Love
> That never will let go.

[11] Taken from: *The Lifted Lamp* by Grace Noll Crowell. Copyright by Harper & Brothers—1942. Used by permission.

This was the faith that enabled John Wesley to cry when his eyes grew dim and earthly anchors were slipping, "The best of all is, God is with us!" This faith led Paul to affirm as he faced the terrors of violent death: "I shall rejoice. . . . As it is my eager expectation and hope that I shall not be at all ashamed, but that with full courage now as always Christ will be honored in my body, whether by life or by death. For to me to live is Christ, and to die is gain." (Phil. 1:19, 20-21.)

Christ was his security, his resource, his rock. The inspired words of Frederick W. H. Myers describe his great witness, which countless others share:

> Christ, I am Christ's and let the name suffice you;
> Aye, for me, too, it greatly has sufficed.
> Lo, with no winning words would I entice you,
> Paul hath no honour and no friend but Christ.
>
> Yea, through life, death, through sorrow and through sinning,
> Christ shall suffice me, for He hath sufficed;
> Christ is the end, for Christ was the beginning,
> Christ the beginning, for the end is Christ.

Productive Peace in Action

The fruit of the Christ Spirit is still peace. Here and there in our own confused and troubled day are found a few serenely confident souls. Tired mothers and weary laborers, statesmen, business and professional men in positions of great responsibility, are going on their way serenely and purposefully, surrounded in this high-speed day by friends who are cracking up and going to pieces under the strain. While their friends are compromising with the right, manipulating their consciences, and fighting themselves and their fears, they are calmly doing what they believe best for all concerned. Most of us know a few people like that, who are holding their homes and communities and nations together. They are at peace because they are sure of God in Christ. "Christ shall suffice me, for He hath sufficed!"

A dramatic testimony of the Spirit's gift of serenity with concern is found in the words of Judge Harold Medina in the article "Someone Else on the Bench." Judge Medina is the distinguished jurist who won fame by his handling of the long and difficult case of the eleven Communist leaders in New York in 1949. He describes the experience which was the secret of his success as a judge. The experience came after several disturbing and frustrating days as he began to learn through prayer and worship that there was Someone beside him on the bench.

"The mysterious presence makes itself felt in every trial in my courtroom," he writes. "It is as if Someone is always watching me, urging me to make sure that my rulings are conscientious and merciful. More and more I come to realize that my acts will be futile unless each one fits into the moral law which governs all."

In describing the tumultuous days of the Communist trial, he wrote, "It took me a long time to realize what the Communists were trying to do to me—to wear me down until I lost my self-control and occasioned a mistrial. But as I felt myself getting weaker and weaker, and found the burden more and more difficult to bear, I sought strength . . . from the one Source that never fails."

Toward the end of August, when the uproar and confusion of the Communists was so distracting, he finally had to leave the courtroom and lie down in his chambers.

Let me be frank: I was thinking then that perhaps I should never go back. In my weakness it seemed to me at last that I had stood as much as I could for as long as I could. I could not endure more of it. I was ready to give up.

But, instead, . . . I asked God to take charge of things and that His will be done. I cannot report any mysterious or supernatural experience as a result of that prayer. All I know is that, as I lay on the couch in the heat of that darkened chamber, some kind of new strength seemed to flow into my veins. . . . After 15 minutes I was refreshed, and went back to carry on the business of my court.

And I gained in strength from that moment on to the end. For Someone else was with me, all the way.[12]

Such calm winners in the battle against the bewildering insecurities of our day belong in the magnificent succession of triumphant souls like Paul, Augustine, Martin Luther, John Wesley, Abraham Lincoln, Albert Schweitzer, Florence Nightingale, and Muriel Lester. They learned after much sad and costly experience, not that peace of soul is something to be earned or deserved, but that it is truly a gift of God. "We are not here to work," says Emerson, "but to be worked upon." We are well, whole, happy, and creative when we learn how to let the divine energies flow through us. Great spirits in every age have spoken of themselves as channels or agents through which inspiration and insight, courage and fortitude, are given. Whether they used the words or not, they were confessing to the reality of the Holy Spirit of God in the life of man.

"It isn't from me," said Haydn, the great musician, as he listened to one of his own compositions, marveling at its grandeur. "It is from above." And Handel, as he heard the "Hallelujah Chorus" for the first time, cried out that it seemed to him as if heaven had been opened.

"All productivity of the highest kind is in no one's control," declared Goethe, the famous poet and writer of the Enlightenment, "but is elevated above all earthly power. . . . I myself am merely a vessel found worthy to receive the divine influence."

When matters were at their worst during the Civil War, Secretary Stanton said to President Lincoln, "I don't see why it is that you are so calm. When everything is going wrong, our generals are losing battles, and we can hear the thunder of guns here in Washington, you seem to keep calm and poised. How do you do it?"

"Well, it's like this, Stanton," Mr. Lincoln replied: "when you feel you are only a pipe for Omnipotence to sound through, you do not worry very much."

When one considers himself a "pipe for Omnipotence to sound

[12] *Reader's Digest*, Aug., 1951. Used by permission of the author and of *Reader's Digest*.

through," as Lincoln thought of himself, the strains and tensions that produce anxiety are quickly lifted. When our securities are in the eternal, the threats of evil men, of physical suffering, and of death, in any time, are presented in their proper proportions. "With the Lord on my side," cried the Psalmist, "I do not fear." (Ps. 118:6.) The fickleness of fame and fortune are no longer objects of undue concern. We learn to say with Browning's Patriot as he was being led to his death down the same street where a few months before to the acclaim of the multitude he had ridden in triumph:

> Paid by the world, what dost thou owe
> Me?—God might question; now instead,
> 'Tis God shall repay: I am safer so.

There is a very close connection between the hour in Martin Luther's study in the little university town of Wittenberg when he began to experience the meaning of Paul's phrase "The just shall live by faith," and the hour before the Diet of Worms. With the might and power of the Holy Roman Empire and the pontiffs and prelates of the medieval church arrayed solidly against him, Martin Luther stood with majestic calmness and fearless courage to declare, "My conscience is captive to the Word of God. I cannot and I will not recant anything . . . God help me. . . . I cannot do otherwise!" Throughout the critical years that followed he continued confidently in his purpose to proclaim the truth. Fear of death—or what was worse, fear of the harm that might come to his beloved Katherine and his little son, Hans Luther—did not move him. Of course he loved his family, but his confidence in God included their welfare even if the worst did happen.

"For to me to live is Christ." This is the freedom from the curse of "this death"—from any and all of the seven deadly sins. This is the secret of serenity with concern as I receive the gift of the Spirit enabling me to be my true self, to possess love that lasts and heals and lifts, and that keeps the sting out of pleasures and things and death.

Conquering the Seven Deadly Sins

FOR ME TO LIVE IS CHRIST

O Christ of the simple life,
　Give me thy simplicity,
　That I shall cease longing for a greatness
　　That is not my own,
　And want only to be the strong, loving person
　　I was meant to be.

O Christ of the agape love,
　Give me thy lovingkindness
　That is moved with compassion toward others
　　And that forgets
　All self-ambitions that curse me.

O Christ of the tender heart,
　Let my heart be broken and touched
　By the misery of those who sit
　　In prison houses of self,
　And give me power to open the doors
　　Of their prisons.

O Christ of the great understanding,
　Make my heart understanding, too.
　Give me new eyes for the unseen
　　In thy universe and in others.
　Make me a glass, though stained, through which others
　　May see the white radiance of eternity.

O Christ of the eternal hope,
　Give me of thy expectancy,
　That, tiptoe, I shall live life
　　To the last;
　And greet the end with a smile that sees
　　Beyond to a new beginning—and thee.

216

INDEX

217

Index

Heredity, 12
Hitler's pride, 43
Hoarding, 147
Holy Spirit, 24-28, 197-200
  deliverer, 22, 23, 24, 26, 29, 57, 73-81,
    103-4, 121, 147-49, 171
  fruits of the, 46, 49, 57, 69, 73, 81-
    82, 126, 151, 184, 196, 208
  gifts of the, 51-53, 126, 197
  Great Companion, 25, 26, 28, 204-10
  near by faith, 200
  relationship with, 30, 46, 49, 54, 57,
    66-79, 98-99, 114, 130, 143, 151,
    166, 181, 202, 211, 215-16
  in the Trinity, 24-28, 197-200
  witness of, 196, 200
Honesty, 144
Hope
  Christian, 125, 132, 216
  renunciation of, 168
Hopelessness without God, 108, 110,
  160
Horney, Karen, 128
Horton, Walter M., 106
Hound of Heaven, 36, 51
Hugo, Victor, 58
Human limitations, 189
Human nature, 109
Humility, 18, 46, 51, 95
Hysterics, 19

Ibsen, Henrik, 108, 111-13
Idleness, 119
Idolatry, 39
Ignorance, 12
Illness, psychosomatic, 12, 14, 19, 57,
  65
Immaturity, 12-13, 18-19. See also
  self-love, misplaced
Impatience, 93
Impotency, 11-23
Inadequacy, 128, 188-89
Indifference, 108-9
Innocence, 166
Insecurity, 189, 191
Insignificance, 132-33
Integration, 11, 177-87
Intemperance, 176
Intolerance, 41, 58, 62-63, 90-94

Jealousy
  human, 16, 18, 20, 56, 63, 172
  of God, 42-43
Jesus
  life of, 52
  revelation of God, 22, 52
  teaching of, 13, 133, 165, 167, 179,
    181, 194, 204-5
  temptation of, 204
Job, 209, 210
Johnson, Paul E., 65
Joseph in Egypt, 166
Joy
  of becoming and being, 151
  fruit of the Spirit, 153, 209
  Jesus', 153
  sources of, 153-57
Judgment, 113-15
Jung, C. F., 19, 129

Kempis, Thomas à, 135-36
Kierkegaard, Soren, 37, 52, 179
Killing, 84-86, 106
Kindness, 81, 105-6, 216
Kingdom of heaven, 55, 132-35
Kinsey Report, 172-73
Knowledge, 9, 12-13, 19
Künkel, Fritz, 19, 69

Labor troubles, 92
Laws, 16-17, 71
Laziness, 111
Lenin, 91-92
Lewis, C. S., 172
Lies, 84
Life
  abundant, 164
  in Christ, 215-16
  out of death, 32-33, 55, 214-15
  eternal, 13
  failing, 9, 12, 109-11
  good, 155
  losing to find, 209-10
  love of, 15, 162
Lincoln, Abraham, 214-15
Link, Henry C., 41
Loneliness, 24, 32, 59
Love
  agape, 31, 33, 57, 67-70, 105, 121,
    167, 169, 171-75, 216

220

Index